C.1

Tales from the
OREGON
DUCKS
SIDELINE

Brian Libby

Foreword by Joey Harrington

SportsPublishingLLC.com

ISBN 13: 978-1-59670-182-3

Publishers: Peter L. Bannon and Joseph J. Bannon Sr.
Senior managing editor: Susan M. Moyer
Acquisitions editor: John Humenik
Developmental editor: Laura Podeschi
Art director: Dustin J. Hubbart
Dust jacket design: Joseph Brumleve
Interior layout: Kathryn R. Holleman
Photo editor: Erin Linden-Levy

Sports Publishing L.L.C.
804 North Neil Street
Champaign, IL 61820
Phone: 1-877-424-2665
Fax: 217-363-2073
www.SportsPublishingLLC.com

Printed in the United States of America

Library of Congress Cataloging-in-Publication Data

Libby, Brian, 1972-
Tales from the Oregon Ducks sideline / Brian Libby ; foreword by Joey Harrington.
    p. cm.
  Includes index.
  ISBN 978-1-59670-182-3 (hard cover : alk. paper)
  1. Oregon Ducks (Football team)–History. 2. University of Oregon–Football–History. I. Title.
  GV958.U553L53 2007
  796.332'630979531–dc22
                            2007026132

To Don Libby

CONTENTS

FOREWORD

I AM PROUD TO BE A DUCK. This association, however, goes far beyond the fact that I played football for the University of Oregon. In many places your feelings of pride are directly linked to the amount of success you had during your tenure. While at the University of Oregon, our football team won 29 of the 32 games in which I participated and I had a record of 25-3 as a starter. I was blessed to be a part of the most successful recruiting class to ever play for our university, winning back-to-back Pac-10 championships. This success, however, is not what makes me proud to be a Duck.

Autzen Stadium is looked upon by many as one of the toughest places to play in the country, if not *the* toughest. Every Saturday thousands of Duck fans fill the stands to cheer on a team that once boasted the longest home winning streak in the country. The fans at Autzen are among the most passionate in the country, and very few teams walk out without feeling as though they were fighting off more than just the opposing team on the field. This passion, however, is not what makes me proud to be a Duck.

Oregon has been at the forefront of the college football scene for almost two decades. It has become common practice to try to emulate what Oregon is doing on offense. The uniforms, love them or hate them, continue to draw attention and keep the Ducks in the public eye. And the way they market players and promote the program on a national level is unmatched by anyone in the country. This attention, however, is not what makes me proud to be a Duck.

I recently sat with Ahmad Rashad during a University of Oregon basketball game at MacArthur Court. He pointed out where his group of friends used to sit during games at The Pit. His seats were two rows in front of a family that took me under its wing while I was in school. That family also provided a home to former Duck basketball player and current coach Ernie Kent while he was at school during the 1970s. While at the game, I received phone calls from two teammates with whom I played, ran into our sports information director, and still had time to say hello to my favorite member of the Daisy Ducks who was selling fundraiser bingo cards in her usual spot.

This is why I am proud to be a Duck.

More than any place I know, every Duck is part of a family. This association doesn't just stop at the edge of the beautiful campus in Eugene, nor does it involve only those who participated in athletics. It continues to every car with an Oregon sticker driving down the street. It continues to any airport when you pass someone wearing an Oregon hat in the terminal. And it continues to any friend who had a friend who went to school in Eugene.

The Duck greeting is simple, yet understood worldwide. The simple salutation of "Go Ducks!" brings a smile to anyone in this family. As a Duck you know you are part of something special and you know you are always welcome. My name is Joey Harrington, and I am proud to be a Duck.

–JOEY HARRINGTON
FEBRUARY 22, 2007

ACKNOWLEDGMENTS

THIS BOOK WOULD NOT HAVE BEEN POSSIBLE without the many former Oregon players and coaches it was my honor and thrill to interview. Special thanks go to Joey Harrington, whose on-field achievements at Oregon not only are unmatched, but who also wrote this book's foreword. He was refreshingly open, thoughtful, humble, and approachable about his career. Claxton Welch and Ahmad Rashad were also particularly generous with their time and provided key insight for passages about Oregon football throughout the turbulent 1960s and '70s. And to all the antagonistic Beaver fans I encountered while growing up, you've helped inspire the writing of this ode to Ducks football.

My sister, Sara, was tremendously helpful as proofreader and confidante. My dad, a 1966 Oregon grad, passed on to me his love of Ducks football, while my mom patiently endured our screaming and brooding by the TV and radio on many a fall Saturday. Numerous friends and other loved ones have been supportive and influential over the years: Paul and Rosie Wolff, Ned Howard, my grandparents, Joel Dunn (in whose young Ducks fan son, Finlay, I see myself), Reese Sterett, Chad Clark, Michael McHenry, Pat and Hank Smith, Mac Montandon, Adrienne Leverette, Neil Griffiths, and many others.

Most of all, immeasurable gratitude goes to my longtime partner, Valarie Smith, who has ceaselessly nurtured and encouraged my writing career (not to mention everything else I do) with empathy, insight, honesty, and an infectious giggle.

PROLOGUE

"KENNY WHEATON'S GONNA SCORE!"

BEFORE EACH GAME AT AUTZEN STADIUM, the Oregon Ducks' ceremonial entrance onto the football field is preceded by a montage of highlights on the massive "Duck Vision" video screen. Year after year, one moment from the highlight reel always receives the biggest cheers. They play it last as a kind of *pièce de résistance* while the team crowds the tunnel opening, like a jack-in-the-box ready to spring.

This Duck Vision crowd-pleaser was born October 22, 1994, on the same field of play. Oregon had led highly touted rival Washington for virtually the entire game, up 17-13 heading into the final quarter. But with 7:44 left in the game, the Huskies fought back to take their first lead at 21-20.

Worse, on the ensuing kickoff after Washington's touchdown, Oregon returner Patrick Johnson slipped on the turf and was called down at the two-yard line. Even for a field goal, this would have to be a very long drive. History didn't favor Oregon, either. Quarterback Danny O'Neil had never led a successful second-half comeback in 16 previous tries as starter. And against Washington in particular, over the years Oregon had often outplayed their more talented rivals only to see victory slip through their fingers.

Despite the danger of snapping the ball from the two-yard line, where a sack would probably mean a two-point safety for the other team and any turnover a touchdown, the Ducks began with a bold 36-yard O'Neil pass to receiver Dameron Ricketts. "Coach Brooks wanted to be aggressive," O'Neil remembers. "On the sideline before the play, he was saying, 'Let's pass. Let's pass.' So we called a play-action pass there and it got us away from the end zone."

A few plays later, on a critical fourth down, O'Neil dove desperately to reach the first-down marker at the Husky 19 with millimeters to spare. It paid off, though. A few plays later, little-used fullback Duane Jones burst through the line for a 12-yard touchdown run.

Oregon had retaken the lead at 27-21 with 2:40 to play. But that was plenty of time for Washington and NFL-bound quarterback Damon Huard to score a potential winning touchdown. "The emotion in that stadium, you could feel it on the sidelines," recalls Rich Brooks. "It was just a hush in the stands. You're thinking, 'Oh my God, they're going to do it to us again. They're going to break our heart.'"

After the kickoff, Washington quickly drove the length of the field (including a key fourth-down conversion) to reach the Ducks' seven-yard line, their retaking the lead now seemingly almost a foregone conclusion. "I just thought, 'I can't believe this is happening,'" Danny O'Neil adds. "We were so close and then it seemed like it was going to slip away."

But by the end of this game, everything had changed, thanks to Kenny Wheaton and what's now commonly referred to simply as "The Pick."

On first and goal at the seven, Huard spotted receiver Dave Janoski in single coverage on the left sideline against Oregon's redshirt freshman cornerback, Kenny Wheaton. This was just what Washington wanted: to isolate an inexperienced defender one-on-one against one of its receivers.

Coming to Eugene from a close-knit Arizona family, Wheaton had been homesick that year, and Brooks had made a habit of spending extra time with the young defensive back. "He would call me into his office and check on me," Wheaton remembers. "Other guys he didn't do that with as freshmen. But what I still appreciate the most was just that it was always straightforward with Coach Brooks. If you can't get the job done, then you don't play. If you get it done, he doesn't care if you're a freshman or sophomore. You're gonna play."

Besides, Wheaton was worth it. Even on a team that had two All-America cornerbacks in future pros Alex Molden and Herman O'Berry, Wheaton is the one who has become the Ducks' quintessential folk hero. More importantly, though, he had the coach's confidence that day against Washington.

"He reminded me of what Bill Musgrave had done on the other side of the ball as a freshman," Brooks says, referring to the record-breaking former Ducks quarterback who'd led Oregon to back-to-back bowls in 1990-1991 after a 27-year bowl drought. "Kenny was undersized, and he didn't have great foot speed. But in practice he always made plays. He kept picking the ball off against our best receivers."

Wheaton had also spent hours studying Washington game film. He knew what play to expect in this scenario near the end zone—an out pass. Before Huard's pass was even thrown, Wheaton decided to make a play for the ball: to "jump the out" as he put it after the game.

The Huskies were right about one thing on that now famous play. Throwing against Wheaton would indeed yield a game-clinching touchdown. What Washington didn't see coming was a 97-yard interception and touchdown by the freshman wearing green and gold uniform No. 20.

"I was sitting in the stands with my wife," former Ducks quarterback and NFL Hall of Famer Dan Fouts recalls. "Whenever the Huskies came to town there was always this sea of purple in the end zones, and in this game there were also two of them sitting in front of us. After Wheaton scored and the crowd was going wild, I said to my wife, 'You know what the best part of this is?' I pointed to the people in purple and I said, 'They're sitting down. *They're* sitting down. And these two f—ers in front of us? *They're* sitting down!'"

Oregon radio announcer Jerry Allen's call of the play—an emotional narrative of shock and interjection that gives way to wilting disbelief over the course of just a few seconds—is now branded into the memory banks of countless Duck fans the world over:

"Huard drops back to throw the ball, looks left, and it's...*intercepted!* The Ducks have the ball...Kenny Wheaton's gonna *score! Kenny Wheaton's gonna score!* The 30, the 20, to the 10, touchdown...on the interception...the most improbable finish to a football game!"

At the time, though, as Wheaton raced downfield, weaving in and out of punch-drunk Husky offensive players not to be caught on his way to the end zone, Brooks was just hoping he'd down the ball. "I'm standing on the sidelines yelling, 'Get down! Get down!'" he remembers. "I didn't want him to fumble. But he goes right by our bench, cuts back towards midfield, and suddenly there's nobody left."

In 1994, the team was celebrating its 100th anniversary, and with that had come many golden moments, from Rose Bowls in 1916, 1919, and 1958 to continuing rivalries with the likes of Oregon State and Washington. There had been legendary players like Norm Van Brocklin, George Shaw, Mel Renfro, Bob Berry, Dave Wilcox, Dan Fouts, Ahmad Rashad, Lew Barnes, and Musgrave. Coaches such as John Robinson, John McKay, Gunther Cunningham, Bruce Snyder, Norv Turner, and George Siefert also spent time on the sidelines in Eugene as players, coaches, or both.

Yet it's really been after the Ducks' first outright Pacific 10 Conference championship in 1994, set in motion by Wheaton's interception, that the team's most consistent success has come. Counting the rest of 1994 after the Washington game and the ensuing 10 years of play, Oregon amassed 94 wins and 43 losses for a winning percentage of about 69 percent—easily the team's best decade.

During that time, "The Pick" has become folklore for Oregon fans. There are framed lithographs of the play sold as artwork, media stories whenever there's an anniversary, and of course there is the replay, seen infinite times on the Internet, in warped videotapes of the game, and

Kenny Wheaton races downfield after his famous interception.
Image provided by The Oregonian

on Autzen Stadium's humongous Duck Vision screen each home Saturday.

"It's a play that I look at with just...joy," Wheaton says today. "Number one, I think of my team. Just to see the look on their faces and where it took us as a team. Then you think about the fans. I get letters to this day from Duck fans, which shows what fans they are. It makes me feel good to know I was a big part of putting smiles on thousands and thousands of faces."

1

WEBFOOTS IN LEATHER HELMETS
1894-1950

ESTABLISHING A TRADITION

THE FIRST SEASON in the University of Oregon's more than 110-year history wasn't really a season at all. In fact, it was just one game. Led by coach Cal Young, Oregon defeated Albany College by a score of 44-2 on March 24, 1894, in an unmarked field on the Eugene campus. Grover Cleveland was president that year, motion picture film had just been invented, and Coca-Cola sold in bottles for the first time.

Oregon was actually scheduled to begin its inaugural season six months later that fall in 1894, but Young had formed a team by the fall of 1893, practicing an entire year early. If first moves count for anything, let it be known that Oregon's original squad was so eager to get on the field that they played a game six months early.

Speaking of firsts, the name of the inaugural Oregon player to score a touchdown on that afternoon against Albany has been lost to history. But luckily, it was one of many scores that game day. Led by quarterback and team captain Frank Mathews, the team from Eugene enjoyed a 22-0 halftime lead before ultimately winning by 42 points. There were only 13 players on the squad, but Coach Young kept his starters in the whole game to play offense, defense, and special teams. Even in 1894, they had benchwarmers.

An Oregon team photo from 1896.
Image courtesy of Special Collections and University Archives, University of Oregon libraries

As quickly as he conjured Oregon's first team, however, Cal Young was gone, his lifetime coaching record a perfect 1-0. His successor, G.A. Church, took over Oregon's team in the fall of 1894. It's a good thing for Oregon that Young had scheduled that early spring game against Albany College, though, because it turned out to be the team's only victory of the year. Their first opponent that winless fall was Oregon Agricultural College, later to be known as Oregon State, who beat Oregon 16-0. A 12-0 loss to Portland and a scoreless tie with Pacific finished the season. After Church's team failed to win any of its three games or even score a single point, he too left the Oregon sidelines.

But the next year Oregon's fortunes improved considerably. In fact, to this day, 1895 stands as the team's only perfect season: 4-0! Led by new coach Percy Benson, the men from Eugene began by besting their new rivals at OAC in a 46-0 drubbing. Willamette was the next victim, though not an easy one, with a final score of 8-4. (Touchdowns were worth four points and the extra point was a two-pointer.) Oregon's perfect season concluded with a second straight matchup against Willamette, a 6-0 shutout.

Originally, the team was known not as the Ducks, but the Webfoots. Initially, at least, this name didn't refer to waterfowl, but represented those Americans who had traveled the Oregon Trail to settle in fertile valleys west of the Cascade Mountains—an agricultural garden of Eden, but a wet one. The Webfoots' colors, green and yellow, represented the stem and buds of the Oregon grape, the state flower.

DOUBLING THEIR PLEASURE

Oregon had a third new coach, J.F. Frick, to go with its third season. 1896 also helped the Webfoots establish an early lead in the ongoing series with Oregon Agricultural College. Frick's squad played only two college games that year, but both were triumphs over the team from Corvallis: first a 2-0 victory, then an 8-4 win.

The Civil War rivalry has always had a reputation as one of the most bitter in college football, and that was true from the start. When the second game was played in Corvallis, Oregon fans were physically attacked on the sidelines and university officials considered ending the annual series for good. But then again, with three victories in four tries against OAC, why quit while you're ahead? It's a motivation that has endured, as Oregon continues to enjoy a double-digit lead in the all-time series.

Oregon's only loss that year was to a non-college team, the Multnomah Athletic Association Club of Portland, by a 12-6 score. Just as today's floundering small college teams often go on the road against marquee programs with sold-out stadiums to earn needed funds, the 1896 Webfoots agreed to play the Multnomah team to cover the expenses of fielding their two-game season.

HUGO UNDEFEATED

Hugo Bezdek was Oregon's first head coach of enduring success, and the first to come with a pedigree. Born in Prague and raised in Chicago, Bezdek played running back at the University of Chicago for one of football's early legends, coach Amos Alonzo Stagg. In fact, Stagg called Bezdek the best player he had ever had. Stagg also recommended Bezdek as a coach to Oregon, which hired him in 1906.

Bezdek's initial foray as Webfoots coach lasted only a year. In 1906 he led Oregon to a 5-0-1 record, one of only three times the team has ever finished without a loss. After the season, Bezdek quit coaching to attend medical school back in Chicago. It ended up being a short-lived detour, for Bezdek was back coaching for Arkansas a year later. He would return to Oregon in 1913, compiling an impressive 30-10-4 record in five seasons. Most importantly of all, Bezdek guided Oregon to its only Rose Bowl victory of the 20th Century, 14-0 over Pennsylvania on January 1, 1917.

In his final season at Oregon the next year, Bezdek was largely missing in action. After the Rose Bowl, he had signed on to coach professional baseball's Pittsburgh Pirates and intended to hold onto both jobs simultaneously. Predictably, the moonlighting didn't last long and he left baseball. But before the 1918 season commenced, Oregon lost Bezdek anyway. He left to coach the Mare Island Marines, a United States military team, which he also would lead to the Rose Bowl. With World War I raging, the Marines were loaded.

Bezdek didn't just win at Oregon: he introduced numerous innovations, from training table meals for players to a newfangled football strategy called the forward pass.

OREGON'S BIGGEST ROUT

As opponents go, the University of Puget Sound may not be a football powerhouse, but Oregon's 115-0 victory on October 22, 1910, stands as quite an achievement by any measure. The UO team records for scoring and margin of victory will probably never be bested. (Not even against Oregon State.)

The leading player in the blowout was Charles Taylor, who scored an astonishing seven touchdowns. As if that weren't enough, he also kicked all extra points for the team's 14 total touchdowns and even added a field goal. His 52 points in the game is, of course, an Oregon record. On the strength of that game alone, Taylor was listed as an honorable mention member of the All-America team. Maybe if he'd scored more points that day, the young man would have been awarded first-team honors.

FIRST ROSES

When the 1916 Oregon team began its season with a 97-0 annihilation over Willamette, it was a harbinger of success to come. The Hugo Bezdek-coached team pitched shutouts in all but one game, including a 14-0 win over Pennsylvania at the Rose Bowl in a season with seven wins, no losses, and one tie.

Ironically, though, it was the lone game of 1916 in which they gave up points, a still-easy 39-14 victory over California, that essentially helped secure for Oregon the trip to Pasadena. Oregon had equaled Washington for the best record in the Pacific Coast Conference (the forerunner of the Pacific 10), and the two teams' head-to-head matchup ended in a scoreless draw. So conference officials awarded the Webfoots the coveted Rose Bowl invitation based on Oregon's larger margin of victory against their mutual opponent, California.

Pennsylvania was the overwhelming favorite to win the January 1 Rose Bowl game. The Quakers featured a trio of All-Americans that included future National Football League commissioner Bert Bell. Oregon's students had to sell the student-owned bookstore to pay for the team's trip.

But out of this came the University of Oregon's first Rose Bowl triumph. Shy Huntington passed to Lloyd Tegert for the game's first touchdown, and halfback Johnny Parsons' 40-yard run to the one-yard

line set up a second score, made by Huntington on a quarterback keeper. As it had done almost all year, Oregon kept its opponent from scoring a single point.

Half a world away, the Bolshevik revolution was about to turn Russia and the 20th Century upside down. But nobody in Eugene or Portland was too busy worrying just yet—the Ducks were Rose Bowl champions.

"We ran into a batch of football that was a cross between a zip of forked lightning and the roll of a fast freight," Pennsylvania coach Bob Folwell said after the game. "We were licked by a better team. Just let it go at that."

"MIGHTY OREGON"

The lone season that saw Oregon finish with a Rose Bowl win also introduced "Mighty Oregon," the team's fight song. The Webfoots had previously been using the music of "On Wisconsin" with rewritten lyrics. Band director Albert Perfect penned the new tune, and DeWitt Gilbert, then a sophomore at the university, wrote its words:

Oregon our alma mater
We will guard thee on and on
Fellows gather 'round and cheer her,
Chant her glory Oregon
Roar the praises of her warriors
Sing the story Oregon
On to victory urge the heroes
Of our Mighty Oregon

SHY HERO

The first Oregon player to earn a spot on the All-America team was C.A. "Shy" Huntington, who began as a kicker for the Webfoots in 1914 but would go on to lead Oregon to a Rose Bowl victory two years later

Shy Huntington, Oregon's first All-American.
Image courtesy of Special Collections and University Archives, University of Oregon libraries

Oregon's coaches receive a good luck charm in Pasadena before the 1919 Rose Bowl.
Image courtesy of Special Collections and University Archives, University of Oregon libraries

as quarterback and defensive back. In the January 1, 1917, contest against Pennsylvania, Huntington picked off four Quakers passes, threw for one Oregon touchdown, and ran for the other.

In 1918, Huntington took over from Hugo Bezdek as head coach. While Oregon officials tried to lure Bezdek back to Eugene numerous times, Huntington put together an impressive tenure of his own with a six-season record of 26-12-6. In 1919, the team's first at Hayward Field (where it would play through 1966), Huntington guided Oregon to its second Rose Bowl appearance, losing 7-6 to Harvard.

Although the Webfoots were held without a touchdown in the nation's only bowl game that year, Huntington's brother Hollis was the key player in the 1919 Rose Bowl, rushing for 122 yards on 29 carries.

An apparent go-ahead Oregon field goal by Skeet Manerud was close enough to fool the scoreboard operator, who prematurely changed the score to 9-7 Webfoots. But the kick was ruled just wide. Shy Huntington would never get Oregon back to Pasadena again, but he remains the team's premier combination of player and coach.

NOT EXACTLY NOTRE DAME

Although familiar teams like Stanford, Washington, USC, and Oregon Agricultural College (later Oregon State) were regulars on the Oregon football schedule during the 1910s and '20s, there was also an eclectic group of squads whose names have not stood the test of time. Many weren't even colleges at all.

Between 1897 and 1905, Oregon played the Chemawa Indians on five occasions. Years 1899 and 1900 featured matchups against a team called Ashland Normal. Pendleton High School was a 1901 opponent, as was Oregon Medical School (convenient for injuries) in 1902. Between 1903 and 1913, the Webfoots even regularly faced off against their own Oregon Alumni team.

In later years, even as college football became more restricted to colleges, Oregon confronted many teams that would eventually cease play. On Halloween in 1931, Oregon faced a heavily favored New York University team at Yankee Stadium. The Ducks defeated the mighty Violets 14-6. Closer to home, Oregon also fed on small colleges, such as Whitman and Linfield, that would play several divisions down in years ahead.

WINS BUT NO BOWLS

Following Shy Huntington's departure after the 1923 season, Oregon's next two coaches—Joe Maddock and Richard Smith—lasted only one year each. But John McEwan finally returned the team to stability and, eventually, winning. An Army captain, McEwan had been an All-America player at West Point in 1914 and its head coach from 1923-1925. For a West Coast school like Oregon, his hiring was a coup.

(Incidentally, one of McEwan's assistant coaches was Eugene Vidal, the father of author Gore Vidal.)

In 1926, McEwan added to the team Oregon's first two African-American players, Robert Robertson (a quarterback) and Charles Williams. But the team posted a disappointing 2-4-1 record both that year and in 1927. Also in 1927, Oregon officially made green and yellow the team's only uniform colors—dropping the occasional use of blue.

McEwan's 1928 team went 9-2, marking the first time Oregon had amassed nine victories in a season. (It took until the year 2000 to get 10.) Led by its new star, sophomore quarterback John Kitzmiller, Oregon's 45-0 win over Pacific in the opening game equaled the cumulative scoring total from the previous seasons' seven contests combined. The 1928 Webfoots also ended a three-year losing streak to the Beavers of OAC, winning 12-0 at Bell Field in Corvallis.

Unfortunately for Oregon, a 9-2 record still wasn't good enough to win the Pacific Coast Conference in 1928. And in those days the Rose Bowl was the only postseason bowl game in which PCC teams competed. This would be the first of many talented Oregon squads to stay home for the holidays.

The 1929 team finished with an impressive but slightly disappointing 7-3 record, given the highly touted Kitzmiller's return and media predictions that the team would challenge for the conference crown. A 14-0 win over Washington that year provided one of Oregon's most memorable all-time plays, not to mention a foreshadowing of Kenny Wheaton's famous interception against the Huskies 65 years later. Washington had driven to Oregon's five-yard line when Oregon defender Bobby Robinson intercepted a pass and raced toward the goal line with no defenders close enough to catch him. But a Washington player on the bench, Larry Westerweller, ran onto the field and tackled Robinson short of the end zone. Officials then awarded the Webfoots the winning touchdown.

Oregon finished 1929 with a cross-country train trip to play Florida in a game that remains to this day the only meeting between the Ducks and Gators. The home team underdogs in Gainesville ended McEwan's career with a 20-6 win over the visitors from Eugene.

THE FLYING DUTCHMAN

John Kitzmiller had a knack for making dramatic defensive plays—hence his nickname, "The Flying Dutchman." As a sophomore in Oregon's first-ever meeting against UCLA in 1928, Kitzmiller returned an interception 96 yards for a touchdown. He also kicked for the team and, in an era of two or (in this case) three-way players, he made his biggest impact as a quarterback.

As starting signal caller in 1928, Kitzmiller led the conference in scoring with 48 points. The next year, a broken leg against the Beavers would keep him out of the team's last three games, but only after overseeing a 16-0 Civil War victory.

As a senior, Kitzmiller led Oregon to a third straight winning season, highlighted by a victory over Drake at Chicago's Soldier Field in one of college football's first night games. Attention from that game helped Kitzmiller earn second-team All-America honors. All told, Oregon would amass a 23-7 record when he was in the lineup, enough to earn Kitzmiller a spot in the College Football Hall of Fame in 1969.

BOWERMAN JUST DOES IT

In 1931, the Ducks were struggling amidst a scoreless deadlock on the road against Washington. But Bill Bowerman, who would later become Oregon's track coach and co-founder of athletics giant Nike with Phil Knight, broke the game open on a record 87-yard punt return for a touchdown. As Bowerman raced downfield with the ball, he was matched step for step on the sidelines by Oregon's then-track coach, 63-year-old Bill Hayward, who shouted to his protégé to keep his knees high. The touchdown made the difference in the game as the Ducks bested the Huskies 7-0.

THE MIDNIGHT EXPRESS

Oregon's 1931 team starred quarterback Leighton Gee and a trio of running backs: Mark Temple, Joe Lillard, and Mike Mikulak, otherwise known as the "Midnight Express."

Lillard didn't stay in Eugene long. He became ineligible after it was discovered he'd played semi-pro baseball under an assumed name. But Lillard would go on to become one of the first two African Americans to play professional football, staying two seasons with the Chicago Cardinals.

Although the Midnight Express grabbed the headlines, another Oregon player became only the school's second first-team All-American that year: tackle George Christensen. But who better to be honored than a lineman who helped make the backfield famous?

TOO "TUFFY" FOR EUGENE

One of the most accomplished football players ever to play for Oregon was Alphonse "Tuffy" Leeman, who would later become an NFL Hall of Famer. But Leeman never did much as a Webfoot. He played only one season, 1932, then transferred to George Washington. It was certainly Oregon's loss, though. Leeman became the MVP of the 1936 College Football All-Star game and led the NFL in rushing as a rookie for the New York Giants, ultimately becoming one of only 11 players to have his jersey retired by the pro team.

PRINK OF SUCCESS

Former two-time all-conference Oregon center Prink Callison had earned the nickname "60-Minute Man" for his relentless play. After an apprenticeship leading the UO freshman squad, which lost only twice in three years during his coaching tenure, Callison led Oregon's varsity to winning records in each of his first four seasons, including annual victories over Oregon State. Unfortunately, though, his final two seasons in Eugene were losing ones. But that's not what sent him packing. "Prink Callison had come up from Medford," recalls Gerald

Calhoun, who played end for the team. "He was only about four years older than us. He was a pretty nice guy, but he had a problem with alcohol. He lost his job over that."

AN UNOFFICIAL SUGAR BOWL WIN

After amassing a 5-3-1 record in 1932, Oregon was invited to play Southeastern Conference champion Louisiana State for an exhibition on December 17 in Baton Rouge. Although it has never been listed as a bowl game for either team, the matchup was a forerunner to the Sugar Bowl, which began in 1935. More than a thousand Oregon fans traveled across the country to Louisiana for the game, with temperatures well below freezing. The Ducks would not be deterred, however, defeating the LSU Tigers 12-0. "We only had about 33 that went on that trip," recalls Calhoun. "But we had about seven different guys who played in the pros. It was a great season."

CONFERENCE CHAMPS, BUT NO ROSES

The 1933 squad earned a share of the conference championship, but didn't get a Rose Bowl trip. Led by fullback and linebacker Mike Mikulak, as well as quarterback Maurice Van Vliet (who would head the Canadian Olympic Committee several years later), Oregon rattled off eight straight victories to begin the season, including a hard-fought 13-3 win at Multnomah Stadium in Portland against Oregon State. But USC tamed the Ducks in Los Angeles a week later. It was not the men of Troy who earned the Rose Bowl berth over Oregon, though, but Stanford.

THE ORIGINAL "IRON MIKE"

The youngest member of Oregon's famous "Midnight Express" backfield of 1931, freshman fullback Mike Mikulak, would go on to become one of the team's most accomplished players. Known as "Iron Mike" long before Chicago Bears player/coach Mike Ditka, Mikulak was Oregon's principal ball carrier for the talented 1932 and '33 teams, as well as a hard-hitting middle linebacker. In 1933, he became a first-team All-American, and two years later achieved all-pro status for the Chicago Cardinals. In those days, however, the NFL was not the glamorous, high-paying league it is today; Mikulak cut short his pro career to become an Oregon assistant coach in 1937.

RECEIVING IN MORSE CODE

The 1934 season was up and down for Oregon, with a 6-1 record giving way to 6-4 after three straight losses at the year's end. But with it came a milestone of sorts, from which Ducks end Raymond Morse was the first of many beneficiaries.

Until that time, teams were penalized five yards for any incompletion after first down. It made throwing the ball too risky much of the time. But the now ridiculous-sounding rule was abolished in 1934, and Oregon adapted immediately with a greater emphasis on passing. Morse caught many passes that season and had three touchdowns, enough to make him the third player from Eugene to be named first-team All-America. "It was different," remembers Gerald Calhoun, who blocked for Morse. "The passing game was nil compared to today. If it was a 10- or 15-yard pass, it was a big deal."

OLIVER'S TWIST

Former West Point player Tex Oliver began the first of two Oregon coaching tenures in 1938, lasting four years before taking the reins again in 1945 after World War II. The coach helped nudge Oregon toward the more pass-oriented game that was already beginning to overtake football's old notions of three yards and a cloud of dust. With the Great Depression still raging, most fans wanted a little entertainment with the game. Oliver's teams did just that, spreading out with new formations and putting the ball in play. He was an originator of the man-in-motion formation. Still, none of Tex Oliver's six seasons brought positive records. By 1946, the administration wasn't asking Oliver for more.

LOSSES IN PERSPECTIVE

On December 6, 1941, Oregon suffered one of its most lopsided defeats in team history, 71-7, to Texas. But it was all forgotten by the next morning. Americans woke to the news that Japan had bombed Pearl Harbor and the country was entering World War II.

Oregon would finish the 1941 campaign and continue for an additional year, but did not field a football team for the 1943 and 1944 seasons. Too many of its players were off fighting. Students were left with only an amateur team made of ROTC students called the "Armyducks." They were coached by former Oregon player John Warren, who had also filled in as coach of the varsity team in 1942 after Tex Oliver, already a World War I veteran, re-enlisted. Unfortunately, the football field was a veritable Waterloo for the amateur Armyducks, who were winless in four games, including two losses to a coastal Coos Bay-based army cavalry unit.

LET THERE BE LEICHT

Oregon's football team returned in 1945 with a mix of war veterans in their mid-to-late 20s and young recruits in their teens. Many veterans weren't back until mid-season, but along with them came a handful of transfer players who had already enjoyed success on other teams before the war.

One such player, Jake Leicht, had already played in the 1944 Cotton Bowl the year before he came to Oregon. In that game, Leicht's Randolph Field Army team shockingly tied the mighty Texas Longhorns. In his sophomore season in 1945 (his first at Oregon), Leicht led the Ducks in rushing, passing, and scoring on offense, and set a team record with 10 interceptions on defense, which also led the nation. He was named first-team All-America, but unfortunately, Oregon finished only 3-6 that year and 4-4-1 the next.

In 1947, however, the mood in Eugene improved considerably with a 7-3 campaign under new coach Jim Aiken and the school's first athletic director, Leo Harris (for whom a parkway outside Autzen

Stadium is now named). Then a senior, Leicht led the Pacific Coast Conference in both rushing and scoring. By the time he graduated, he owned team records for single-season and career interceptions as well as punt returns.

Incidentally, 1947 is also noteworthy for the agreement made between Harris and Walt Disney. Their handshake that year allowed Oregon to use a version of Donald Duck as its mascot.

By this time, even All-American Leicht was becoming overshadowed by Oregon's new quarterback, Norm Van Brocklin, who led the team in passing in 1947. Former coach Tex Oliver had only used Van Brocklin sparingly and as a running back earlier in his career. "He's only a fair runner and he can't block," the coach had said in his evaluation. True as these weaknesses may have been, Oliver failed to notice he had a future NFL Hall of Fame passer on his hands. Luckily the next Oregon coach, Aiken, didn't make the same mistake.

PULLING RANK

The Oregon Ducks made their first-ever appearance in the Associated Press writers' poll on October 26, 1948, ranked 14th following a 33-7 victory over Washington State. It was really the week before, though, that the team cemented its reputation, upsetting USC at Multnomah Stadium in Portland. After closing out the regular season with wins over Washington, UCLA, and Oregon State, the Ducks would climb all the way to ninth before a New Year's Day loss to Southern Methodist in the Cotton Bowl. It became the highest ranking for the team until the Ducks reached No. 7 halfway through 1964, and one of only nine seasons (prior to 2006) in which Oregon has cracked the top 10 in either the AP writers or United Press International (later *USA Today* and ESPN) coaches' poll.

Quarterback Norm Van Brocklin, Oregon's first
player inducted into the Pro Football Hall of Fame.
Image courtesy of Special Collections and University Archives, University of Oregon libraries

THE RISE OF NORM VAN BROCKLIN

The tradition of great quarterbacks at the University of Oregon in football's modern era of passing begins with Norm Van Brocklin. After serving in World War II from 1943-1945 and warming the bench as a freshman, he only compiled two years as starter: 1947 and '48. During that time he established himself as arguably the best college football quarterback in America. Oh, and he punted on a few necessary occasions, too.

An early 1-3 record in 1947 may have shown the inexperience of young South Dakota-born, California-raised Norman Mack Van Brocklin—that, and the fact that Oregon was breaking in the new "T" formation. But Van Brocklin and the team soon rallied, rattling off six straight wins, including a 14-6 victory over Oregon State, to end the season.

Although Van Brocklin was all-conference that year along with Jake Leicht, it was really in 1948 that he shined. Oregon amassed a 9-1 record, its only loss a non-conference defeat on the road against mighty Michigan en route to the Cotton Bowl.

Van Brocklin decided to forgo his senior season at Oregon after earning his degree in three years. But he was just getting warmed up in football. Selected by the Los Angeles Rams, he played 12 seasons. Highlights from his career included two NFL championships (with the Rams and Eagles), nine Pro Bowls, and a Most Valuable Player trophy after his final campaign in 1960. Afterward, Van Brocklin was a head coach for 13 seasons with Minnesota and Atlanta. He was inducted into both the Pro Football Hall of Fame and the College Hall of Fame. Years later, *The Eugene Register-Guard* would name Van Brocklin the school's all-time quarterback.

Not bad for a guy whose original Ducks coach made him a third-string halfback.

BEFORE HE COACHED, HE RAN

John McKay is a legendary name in the annals of college and pro football history, having guided the USC Trojans to four national championships before taking the NFL expansion Tampa Bay Buccaneers from laughingstock to Super Bowl contender in a handful of years. McKay first turned heads at Oregon, where, as a running back in 1948 and '49, he set a team record for most yards per carry (6.1) that still stands today.

Of course, McKay had help. His quarterback was the great Norm Van Brocklin. Fellow running backs George Sanders, Bob Sanders, and talented Woodley Lewis (whose kick return records still stand) also shared the load carrying the ball. McKay was a speedy, shifty tailback whose style complemented the other backs' power.

Immediately after his playing days ended, a young McKay took up the coaching profession, becoming an assistant with the Ducks from 1950-1958. Although he would go on to greater glory elsewhere, John McKay first nurtured his football genius in Eugene.

THE 1949 COTTON BOWL

Led by Van Brocklin, Oregon was a perfect 7-0 in Pacific Coast Conference play in 1948, but the team lost out to 6-0 California for the PCC's Rose Bowl berth. The Ducks and Bears didn't play each other that year in the usual tiebreaker. Instead, conference representatives— one from each team—voted for Cal 7-3, with Oregon reportedly earning votes from Oregon State and Washington State, but not Washington. Some would argue it was after this regional disloyalty that the Ducks-Huskies rivalry first started to turn bitter. Van Brocklin unabashedly shed tears at an Oregon Club event upon hearing the news his team wasn't going to Pasadena.

This wasn't the first time Oregon had narrowly missed out on the Rose Bowl, but unlike previous seasons when it meant staying home, the Ducks were able to play in a bowl anyway. After briefly considering two other postseason contests—a non-bowl exhibition with Oklahoma

Oregon (dressed in white) battles SMU in the 1949 Cotton Bowl.
Image courtesy of Special Collections and University Archives, University of Oregon libraries

in Los Angeles and the Harbor Bowl in San Diego—Oregon finally received an invitation to play Southwest Conference champion SMU in a marquee January 1 game: the Cotton Bowl.

The contest began with SMU driving 73 yards on its first possession for a one-yard touchdown by Heisman Trophy winner Doak Walker. After a scoreless second quarter, the Mustangs added to their 7-0 halftime lead with a 36-yard touchdown run by halfback Kyle Rote.

Trailing 14-0 in the third quarter, the Ducks came alive. Van Brocklin would finish 6-for-10 in second-half passing, equaling Walker's total for the game. The Oregon quarterback found Dick Wilkins for a 24-yard pass early in the fourth period, but the momentum was quickly taken back by SMU with a third touchdown (by a man named Chicken

Roberts, no less) with 8:45 left. Oregon scored again when Van Brocklin found Darrell Robinson for a 41-yard touchdown pass to make it 21-14. But SMU held on as the final six minutes went by without any further scoring.

The Ducks led the Mustangs in total yardage, and Van Brocklin shook off a slow start to look every bit the superstar he'd been to fans in Eugene for the last two years. But the Ducks would have to wait another 12 years for their first bowl win since the 1916 Rose Bowl.

Coach Jim Aiken's first two years had seen Van Brocklin guiding the team to an impressive 16-5 overall record, with only the team's third-ever New Year's Day bowl appearance. But after Van Brocklin's departure, the team suffered two straight losing seasons, including a disastrous 1-9 campaign in 1950, the year President Harry Truman approved production of the hydrogen bomb and sent combat troops to Korea. Under pressure from the university's administration, Aiken resigned in June 1951. There had been rumors of improprieties, but Aiken's nerves were also shot. "I remember after we lost the Iowa game seeing him sitting by himself behind the bleachers," recalls John Gram, a student manager for the team that year. "He was smoking a cigarette, and his hands were just shaking."

Aiken's tenure was also overshadowed by Oregon's next coach, Len Casanova, who would stay for 16 seasons and finally take the Ducks back to Pasadena. But give Jim Aiken his due for molding an all-time great in Van Brocklin and producing one of Oregon's best two-year runs.

2

CASANOVA'S CHARMS
1951-1966

THE COMING OF 'CAS'

WHEN THE SEARCH FOR A NEW COACH commenced, a member of the Portland Duck Club began campaigning for his former high school coach, Len Casanova, who was unhappy after his first season with the Pitt Panthers. Before that, Casanova had led tiny Santa Clara to an unlikely Orange Bowl win over Kentucky in 1950. He longed to be back in the West, and accepted the Oregon job despite inheriting a team that had been depleted by Korean War enlistments and lacked talent.

It took time for "Cas," as he was familiarly known, to turn the Ducks program around. His first two years were lean ones, with just a pair of victories each season. After a mediocre 4-5-1 campaign in 1953, though, his team began to roll. Four straight winning seasons culminated in the 1958 Rose Bowl, in which Oregon fell just three points short of upsetting No. 1 ranked Ohio State. There would be two more bowl appearances later, and finally a win to end the bowl drought dating back to 1916. Long after Casanova's 16-year coaching career ended, he would remain a fixture on the Oregon campus, first as athletic director and later as a retired father figure to some of the coaches who succeeded him.

In his first years at Oregon in the early 1950s, though, Casanova went about the steady, unglamorous task of making winners one tackling drill at a time. As much as practice or athletic ability, the integrity and goodwill underscoring the entire program set coach Len Casanova's teams apart. Players knew Cas and his staff respected and cared about them as men. From that trust, they built a winning program that often went toe-to-toe against teams with far greater resources and talent.

LEARNING TO WIN

In 1953, Len Casanova's third season in Eugene, the Ducks were still a year away from a winning record. But the season began with an impressive victory on the road over college football powerhouse Nebraska. The game was also the first-ever nationally televised "Game of the Week" on NBC. Played on September 19, game-time temperatures in Lincoln were hot and humid, but the Ducks stunned the Cornhuskers 20-12 behind quarterback George Shaw, whose star would rise prominently over the next year.

Perhaps the historic victory took a little too much out of Oregon. The team proceeded to lose four in a row, although one more upset remained that year against No. 4 ranked USC in Portland. In that contest, Oregon scored less than a minute into the game on a trick play when second-string quarterback Barney Holland passed to Shaw for a touchdown. At game's end, with USC in striking range for a go-ahead touchdown, Oregon preserved its 13-7 lead thanks to a Dick James interception.

Young, inexperienced teams with talent often suffer Jekyll-and-Hyde seasons, winning impressively one week and falling apart the next. In the transitional year of 1953, Casanova's team was stopped short of a winning season by one game, but showed the increasingly talented Ducks could, for the first time since Norm Van Brocklin's departure five years earlier, compete with the nation's top teams.

HE CAME, HE SHAW, HE CONQUERED

Imagine today if a college football player led the NCAA in interceptions as a freshman and three years later was named its total offense leader. It would be almost unthinkable. But George Shaw did it all at Oregon in the early 1950s. He also played receiver, running back, and kicked field goals. During football's off-season, this incredibly versatile athlete was also an All-America baseball player.

In 1951, normally a time when freshmen didn't even play, Shaw amassed a stunning 13 interceptions. (The next closest in Oregon's record book is just nine, achieved by Steve Smith exactly 50 years later.) Shaw's first season as an established starting quarterback, a 4-5-1 campaign in 1953, included not only upsets over Nebraska and USC, but also a 26-13 win against San Jose State in which he threw for one touchdown and caught a pass for another.

As a senior, Shaw set both team and conference passing records with 1,536 yards while giving Len Casanova his first winning season in Eugene at 6-4. Shaw's duel with Stanford quarterback and future San Francisco 49ers Hall of Famer John Brodie resulted in a 13-18 defeat. But two weeks later the Oregon signal caller bested another hot Bay Area quarterback, Cal's Paul Larson, in a close 33-27 win.

Shaw also helped Oregon end losing streaks to Washington and Oregon State, passing for three touchdowns during his final game in a Ducks uniform, a 33-14 Civil War triumph.

In 1955, Shaw was a first-round draft choice of the NFL's Baltimore Colts, but eventually lost the starting job to legendary quarterback Johnny Unitas. Over seven seasons in the league, though, Shaw would go on to pass for just under 6,000 yards with the Colts, New York Giants, Minnesota Vikings, and Denver Broncos.

BEAVERS BE DAMMED

November 20, 1954, capped a season of sweet relief for Oregon. After five straight losing seasons and five straight losses to the Beavers, the Ducks bested their Corvallis rivals 33-14 for Len Casanova's first

Civil War coaching victory in four tries. "This, at long last," wrote L.H. Gregory in *The Oregonian*, "was Oregon's football day."

Trailing the Beavers 7-0 after one quarter, the Ducks capitalized on three Oregon State turnovers with three touchdowns—the first on a Jasper McGee run and the next two on passes from quarterback George Shaw, playing in his last game for the Ducks—in a less than seven-minute span before the half.

In the second half, Shaw handed off to McGee for another score and also connected on a 52-yard touchdown pass to Dick James, who tied John Kitzmiller for the team's season scoring record with 66. The 19-point victory was the largest Civil War winning margin since Oregon's 27-0 victory en route to the 1916 Rose Bowl.

GROUND DUCK

After Shaw graduated to the NFL, Oregon depended largely on its ground game. Running backs Dick James and Jack Morris made it a ground attack by committee, but the team's leading ball carrier in this mid-'50s period was Jim Shanley, who would end his career as Oregon's all-time leader in rushing, scoring, and total yards.

As a sophomore in 1955, Shanley was ranked 10th in the country with 711 yards. It was an up-and-down year for the team, though, with three straight losses followed by four straight wins. After a blowout late-season loss to Stanford left the Ducks 5-4, a group of Oregon students caused a stir on campus by hanging coach Len Casanova in effigy. But it fired up the team as they rallied around their coach just in time for the Civil War, trouncing Oregon State 28-0. In the snow and mud of Hayward Field, Shanley and quarterback Jack Crabtree each scored two touchdowns, with the Ducks amassing 327 rushing yards for a second straight win against the Beavers.

1956 was largely a disappointment for the 4-4-2 Ducks, with a four-game skid that included a 6-0 loss to UCLA after Shanley's near opening-kickoff touchdown was nullified on a penalty. The highlight, though, was a surprising upset in Portland against USC, who came into the game 6-1. But Oregon's Charley Tourville's three-yard touchdown in the second quarter was the only score in a defensive struggle. When the Ducks tied Rose Bowl-bound Oregon State to end the season, it was a sign that the Ducks were about to more fully realize their potential.

FINALLY, PASADENA BOUND

Len Casanova's 15-year career in Eugene was punctuated by the 1957 season, in which Oregon made its first trip to the Rose Bowl in 39 years (and also its last for another 37 years).

But first, in September the Ducks had to get by Idaho, who came within a field goal of beating Oregon in the season opener, 9-3. The next week was another field-goal battle, this time with Pittsburgh winning 6-3 at Multnomah Stadium in Portland. Then Casanova's team started rolling, shutting out UCLA 21-0 and San Jose State 26-0. Oregon squeaked by Washington State after the Cougars missed a late extra-point attempt. A solid 24-6 beating of California gave way to another one-point squeaker, this time over Stanford.

Ahead in the Rose Bowl race by two games with only three matchups left, Oregon lost to Washington in a turnover-plagued 13-6 contest. But this was thankfully a rare down year for USC, who Oregon blanked 16-0 in Los Angeles. Going into Civil War week, the Ducks and Beavers were the only two PCC teams with a single loss apiece. But the Beavers were ineligible for a Pasadena trip because of the PCC's "no repeat" rule—Oregon State had played there the season before. So Oregon had a Rose Bowl berth clinched before the game.

Good thing for the Ducks, because Oregon State won 10-7 with the help of a controversial referee's call at Hayward Field. Late in the game, Oregon faced a fourth down and goal inside the Beaver one-yard line. Oregon's Jim Shanley appeared to reach the plane of the goal line, but at the same moment Oregon State defender Nub Beamer slapped the ball from his grasp. Officials gave Oregon State the ball. Oregon was still going to the Rose Bowl, but the conference championship would have to be shared with its arch-nemesis.

Oregon prepares to battle #1 Ohio State in the 1958 Rose Bowl.
Image courtesy of Special Collections and University Archives, University of Oregon libraries

Any Big Ten champion would be a tough opponent in Pasadena, but the Ducks had a particularly tall order in facing No. 1-ranked Ohio State. Oddsmakers made Oregon a two- to three-touchdown underdog. But if it's possible to lose and still prove the naysayers wrong, the Ducks did just that on January 1, 1958.

Woody Hayes' Buckeyes scored their only touchdown of the game in the first quarter, which the Ducks equalized in the second on a 10-play, 80-yard drive culminating in Jim Shanley's five-yard run to the end zone. A scoreless third quarter kept it 7-7, but Ohio State notched a field goal a minute into the fourth.

Oregon had its chances to tie or win. First Jack Morris missed a 34-yard field goal attempt with 5:20 left. Another drive saw the Ducks reach OSU's 24-yard line before turning the ball over. The Ducks got the ball back in the game's final minute, but could get no further than Ohio State's 43 as time expired.

Casanova's men bested the Buckeyes in first downs and total yards, but turnovers cost them. Yet players like Shanley, Jack Crabtree, Ron Stover, and Jack Morris could hold their heads high as they headed back to Eugene.

DEFENSE NEVER RESTS

Len Casanova called 1958 his most disappointing in 16 seasons as Oregon's coach. Despite one of the greatest defensive squads in Ducks history, offensive woes saw the team finish 4-6.

After beginning with a 27-0 annihilation of Idaho, the team traveled to Norman, Oklahoma, to play the No. 1-ranked Sooners. Counting the Rose Bowl from the season before, this was the second time in just three games that Oregon would face the nation's top team. And once again, the Ducks played heroically only to come up short, 6-0. Oklahoma's only score came off an Oregon fumble, and the Ducks drove inside the Sooner 30-yard line four times without scoring. Oregon even outgained Oklahoma by more than 100 yards.

After blanking USC 27-0 at Multnomah Stadium in Portland, the dam burst with four straight losses. Yet the 23-6 defeat to eventual Rose Bowl representative California was the only time all season an Oregon opponent scored more than seven points. Unfortunately, Oregon's offense also went scoreless in four contests.

At season's end, following a 20-0 victory over Oregon State, Oregon traveled across the country to play Miami. The Hurricanes' only score was a safety, but the Ducks still lost 2-0. In 10 games, Oregon held its opponents to just 50 total points for the season. Excluding the Cal loss, that's only 27 points in nine games.

SHUNNED BUT THRIVING

In 1959, the Pacific Coast Conference disbanded. USC, UCLA, Stanford, California, and Washington formed a new league, leaving out Oregon, Washington State, and Oregon State. The Ducks had to scramble to put a schedule together after the two Los Angeles schools refused to even honor their planned games. As a result, Oregon actually played Washington State twice that year.

Amidst the uncertainty, Len Casanova compiled an impressive 8-2 record. The Ducks began with five straight victories, including a 21-3 win over an Air Force squad to end the Falcons' 15-game winning streak.

Oregon missed its chance to avenge Washington's Northwest disloyalty when the Huskies squeaked by 13-12 at Multnomah Stadium. After three more wins, Oregon finished the season holding Oregon State without a single completed pass, but Oregon State rallied to win 15-7 at Hayward Field. An 8-2 record would bring a mid-tier bowl game today; in 1959 it meant going home for the holidays.

GIVE THEM LIBERTY

The 1960 Ducks began with a 33-6 victory over Idaho, but the competition got decidedly tougher the next week. Playing at Michigan, the Ducks were shut out 21-0. Yet Oregon's only remaining regular-season loss came by a single point, 7-6, to Washington. As voters headed to the polls to narrowly elect John F. Kennedy over Richard Nixon, the Ducks notched victories over Stanford and West Virginia. A Civil War tie against OSU in Corvallis kept Oregon from matching the previous season's record, but this time, the Liberty Bowl came calling with an invitation to play Penn State in Philadelphia.

Temperatures dipped below freezing for the game, and the sidelines were taken up by huge snow banks that had never melted after more than two feet had fallen the week before. Oregon was cold in more ways than one. Nittany Lions quarterback Dick Hoak ran for two touchdowns, threw for another, and picked off two passes on defense.

Although Oregon led 6-0 after the first quarter on a touchdown run by quarterback Dave Grosz, it was costly, as leading receiver Cleveland Jones was lost for the game to injury. Penn State scored 21 unanswered points in the second quarter to take command, but Oregon narrowed the score to 21-12 on a Dave Grayson touchdown run after halftime. The dam burst, however, as PSU scored another 20 points in the fourth quarter for a 41-12 thrashing.

Nevertheless, this two-year run was one of the Ducks' most successful, with a 15-5-1 mark. Oregon's only losses in these back-to-back campaigns were to archrivals Washington and Oregon State (by a total of 10 points) and to national powers Michigan and Penn State. With all-time Duck greats Mel Renfro and Bob Berry about to matriculate in Eugene, the future looked limitless.

ANOTHER SIDELINE LEGEND

Len Casanova was not only a celebrated coach himself, but he also tutored a number of assistants who would go on to coaching greatness. Unfortunately for Duck fans, two such coaches would lead a mighty conference foe: USC.

The first was Oregon alum John McKay, who, after coming to Los Angeles in 1959, led the Trojans to four national championships and two Heisman Trophies. A year after McKay left Eugene, Casanova added assistant John Robinson, who stayed in Eugene for 11 years before also heading to Troy. Robinson led the Trojans to a share of the 1978 national championship (with Alabama) before bolting like McKay for the NFL, leading the Los Angeles Rams to two NFC title games.

"John Robinson was just a giant," says Claxton Welch, who played running back for Oregon from 1966-1968. "He could break down defenses with the best of them, but he also got the most out of players by supporting and encouraging people. Just like Cas, he took people under his wing."

ALL-EVERYTHING MEL RENFRO

He just might be the greatest player in the more than 110-year history of Oregon football. On offense, Mel Renfro was a running back who could both bowl opponents over or make them miss. He also caught passes and, on occasion, even threw them. On defense (this still being the era of two-way players) Renfro was one of the country's most talented defensive backs, a position he'd play for the NFL's Dallas Cowboys in a 14-year Hall of Fame career. While at Oregon, he earned All-America honors not just in football, but also as a high hurdler in track.

A star athlete at Portland's Jefferson High School, Renfro considered passing up college altogether. "I had been courted a lot but I wasn't really sure I was college material," he recalls. "I knew I was as an athlete, but most of my buddies were finding jobs and going into the service." Even as late as the summer of what would become his freshman year, Renfro hadn't decided.

"I was heavily recruited by Oregon State, and I was leaning towards going there," he recalls. "They were at my doorstep it seemed like every other day. [Future Heisman Trophy winner] Terry Baker was there, and Amos Marsh, who was a football player and track guy—we'd become pretty good friends. But I guess Len Casanova had talked a lot with my parents. My dad asked me where I wanted to go, and I said, 'Oregon State.' And he said, 'No, you're going to Oregon.' And that was that."

Renfro's rushing statistics aren't as impressive as some of the Oregon backs who came afterward, such as Bobby Moore, Derek Loville, or Reuben Droughns. But those statistics are misleading. Renfro absolutely dominated the game on both sides of the ball. In his first game to rush for more than 100 yards versus Idaho as a sophomore in 1961, Renfro gained 122 yards on just four carries. Against Utah the following year, he gained 120 yards on just eight carries.

In perhaps his best game, which came on the road in Houston against Rice, Renfro responded like a champion to adversity in the city where he was born. With segregation still the norm, African Americans

Mel Renfro.
Image courtesy of Special Collections and University Archives, University of Oregon libraries

weren't allowed into the stadium. But an exception was made for about 20 of the player's relatives, who watched from a cordoned-off section at the 40-yard line. "It was the first time my granddad had seen me since I was two years old," Renfro recalls. "I saw him in the stands, and it was an incredible feeling. I think that had a big psychological effect on how I played that day." Renfro rushed 13 times for 141 yards, caught two passes for 27 yards, and returned an interception for another 65 yards as Oregon won 31-12. A Houston newspaper headline the next day read, "Renfro Runs Rice Ragged."

At Stanford in 1963, Renfro had just come back after breaking a bone in his foot. "I touched the ball three or four times and scored three times," he says. "For some reason I always seemed to shine against

Stanford." In that game, Renfro also accomplished a rare trifecta of running, catching, and throwing for touchdowns. While No. 20 wore an Oregon jersey, the halfback pass went from trick play to a regular part of the offense.

All these dominant moments are from just one side of the ball. Renfro's Hall of Fame NFL career would occur entirely on defense, at which he could also dominate while with Oregon. Against Ohio State in 1962, Renfro recorded 15 unassisted tackles with more than 25 overall. He played on every down that game. Like anyone, Renfro had his challenging moments, yet no other football player in Ducks history was so complete.

CASANOVA'S BEST DENIED

Although Len Casanova took Oregon to three bowl games and twice led teams to 8-2 regular seasons, the coach called his 1962 squad, which finished 6-3-1 and did not reach postseason play, his best in a 16-year tenure. Led by Renfro and quarterback Bob Berry, it was certainly one of the most talented.

But Oregon had a particularly brutal schedule that year, with road games against powerhouses Ohio State and No. 1-ranked Texas, as well as a Civil War matchup against OSU and that year's Heisman Trophy winner, Terry Baker. In its first game against Texas, Oregon enjoyed a halftime lead, only to wilt in 90-degree heat and high humidity and let the Longhorns come back for a 25-13 win. "We fumbled early in the third quarter and then we ran out of gas in the heat," Renfro remembers. "That's a game we very easily could have won." Four convincing non-conference victories followed, and after a tie with Washington, Casanova's squad won two more before its only decisive loss of the season—26-7 against Woody Hayes' defending national champion Buckeyes in Columbus.

The Ducks were far more frustrated, though, against Oregon State. Oregon was to receive a Bluebonnet Bowl invitation contingent upon beating the Beavers. The Ducks enjoyed a 17-6 halftime lead on the strength of a 50-yard touchdown pass from Berry to Renfro. In the second half Terry Baker led the Beavers to a touchdown on their first drive, but the Dave Wilcox-led Ducks defense seemed to tighten after that.

Then came perhaps the unluckiest play in Ducks history. On fourth down at the Oregon 34, a short "pooch" punt by Beaver Rich Brooks (the future Duck coach) bounced off the ground at an angle and hit Renfro in the leg. Oregon State recovered, but the Oregon defense again held for three plays. On fourth down, however, Baker passed for the winning score. Baker won both the Heisman and *Sports Illustrated*'s "Sportsman of the Year" award that year, while Oregon was left fuming at a fluke play that had ruined the Ducks' chances for a bowl of their own.

But with the hindsight of history, 1962 turned out to be a season to build on. Casanova's team had just finished the first of what would become three straight winning seasons, a feat that had not been achieved in Eugene for 25 years. And by the next season, those bowl game dreams would no longer go unsatisfied.

THE BERRY GOOD YEARS

It's far from a coincidence that Oregon experienced one of its most fruitful periods during Bob Berry's three years as starting quarterback.

In 1962, Berry helmed a 6-3-1 team that lost only to Ohio State, Texas, and the Beavers. The next season, only Penn State could defeat Oregon when Berry started and finished a game (two losses came with the quarterback injured). Berry, Mel Renfro, and company concluded the year by leading Oregon to its first bowl win in 46 years: the 1963 Sun Bowl. In his senior campaign, Berry guided the Ducks to a 6-0 start and a No. 7 Associated Press ranking. Only a two-point loss to Stanford and a one-point Civil War defeat kept Berry from guiding the Ducks to Pasadena. Berry would get his due, however: The handsome QB with the Beatle-like mop top was named first-team All-America in 1964.

"Berry, I thought, was an excellent leader—very fiery, always up and ready," Mel Renfro recalls. "He was always pushing us. He was also a great communicator. He would ask us, 'What do you think we can do? Can you beat your guy on this play? What do you think will work?' I said, 'Whatever you call, buddy, I'll *make* it work.'"

By the time his career ended in Eugene, Berry was the school's all-time leading passer with just under 4,300 yards. Drafted by Philadelphia, he played in the NFL for nine seasons, principally for the Minnesota Vikings and Atlanta Falcons.

BIG DAVE WILCOX

Amidst the hoopla of Berry and Renfro's offensive heroics at Oregon from 1962-1964, it's easy to forget that Len Casanova's team relied equally on a stout defense led by future NFL Hall of Famer Dave Wilcox. Although he only played two years in Eugene after transferring to Oregon from Boise Junior College, in 1962 and particularly as a senior in '63, Wilcox acted as a key run stopper and pass rusher.

Wilcox's duels with Oregon State quarterback Terry Baker in the 1962 Civil War represent a quintessential one-on-one confrontation in the entire century-plus rivalry. Initially, Wilcox got the better of that year's Heisman winner, sacking Baker two plays in a row to force the late fourth-quarter Beaver punt that would ultimately be recovered by OSU and, on a desperate fourth-down play, the winning touchdown.

In 1963 as Oregon earned a Sun Bowl win and avenged the previous year's Civil War, Wilcox was named the team's most improved player and earned all-conference honors. In the victorious Sun Bowl, Wilcox and Oregon's defense held SMU scoreless for the game's first 50 minutes, including a goal-line stand in the third quarter.

After being named Most Valuable Lineman in the 1964 Hula Bowl, Wilcox was drafted by the San Francisco 49ers, playing in seven Pro Bowls. He was enshrined in the Pro Football Hall of Fame on July 29, 2000.

"I grew up in San Francisco and got to be a ball boy for the team while he was playing," Dan Fouts remembers. "Dave was always a class guy. He kind of epitomizes an Oregon athlete, I think: the strong, silent type that never brings attention upon himself but is a good player."

Two of Dave Wilcox's sons also went on to play for Oregon—tight end Josh Wilcox was a key member of the 1994 Rose Bowl and 1995 Cotton Bowl seasons.

HOOSIER DADDY

Coming into their November 16, 1963, meeting with Indiana at Portland's Multnomah Stadium, Oregon faced a season on the brink. Led by its "Firehouse Four" backfield of Berry, Renfro, receiver Larry Hill, and running back Lu Bain, the team began 4-1 only to suffer a heartbreaking 26-19 loss to Washington in which both Berry and Renfro were knocked out of the game. The next week, Oregon was upset by San Jose State 13-7 as the Spartans scored on an interception and kick return.

Berry and Renfro were still banged up as they strapped on their yellow helmets that afternoon, the quarterback hobbling on a bad knee and running back nursing bruised ribs. The Ducks had never defeated a Big Ten opponent, and when Indiana jumped out to a 13-0 lead, the prospects didn't look promising.

Berry's second-quarter touchdown pass finally put Oregon on the board, and a four-yard Renfro touchdown after halftime gave Len Casanova's team its first lead. (The running back finished with 236 all-purpose yards that day, one of his best performances as a Duck.) The advantage was short lived, though, as Indiana almost immediately pulled back ahead, 19-14. Undeterred, Berry found Hill for a 37-yard touchdown pass to again retake the lead in the final period.

Next it was up to the Oregon defense. Indiana drove to the Ducks' four-yard line, but H.D. Murphy made a key tackle to force the Hoosiers to settle for a field goal. Still, the visitors from Bloomington led 22-21 with just 1:09 remaining in the game.

Murphy wasn't done. After returning Indiana's kickoff to the 25, he caught a pass from Berry to get Oregon's drive moving. Berry's next pass was deflected and almost picked off, but Renfro grabbed it out of the air for a dramatic 30-yard gain to the Hoosier 38. An incomplete pass and an offside penalty left Oregon at the 29 with only 17 seconds remaining. A field goal could win the game, but at 46 yards, the odds were iffy.

With time for perhaps only one more play before trying a kick, Berry dropped back to pass and saw Murphy sprinting down the middle of the field. His pass got there just in time, as Murphy caught the game winner with only a step to spare before going out of bounds. "I didn't think I'd caught it until everybody started grabbing me," Murphy told Eugene's *Register-Guard*. The "everybody" he referred to was not just Oregon players but a mob of jubilant fans.

Unfortunately that joy turned to sorrow six days later, when President John F. Kennedy was assassinated.

SAME SEASON, DIFFERENT WORLD

When the Ducks and Beavers took the field on November 30 after a one-week delay following President Kennedy's death, the intensity of one of college football's most bitter rivalries was put in perspective: Beaver or Duck, they were all Americans in mourning. "I remember we were in class and the professor left the room. He came back and announced that classes were being let out because the president had been assassinated," Mel Renfro recalls. "It just hit you in the pit of your stomach."

As would be the case 38 years later when coach Mike Bellotti's Ducks took the field after the terrorist attacks of September 11, 2001, playing football was ultimately a much-needed diversion. Unfortunately for Oregon, though, star running back Mel Renfro didn't have that chance. The night before the game, he smashed a mirror with his fist and suffered a severe laceration that would require surgery and kept him out of action the next day.

What Oregon did have was a red-hot Bob Berry, who set a new school passing record with 249 yards against Oregon State. After a heartbreaking last-second loss against Terry Baker's Beavers the year before, the Ducks ended suspense early this time around.

After a scoreless first quarter, Berry followed an Oregon field goal with a five-yard touchdown pass to Corky Sullivan and a Lu Bain four-yard score. The 17-0 halftime lead became 31-0 once Bain scored again from 13 yards out and Berry hit H.D. Murphy for a 39-yard touchdown. Two meaningless Beaver scores against Oregon's reserves made it a 31-14 triumph.

"An aroused band of Oregon Ducks," Don McLeod wrote in *The Oregonian*, were "generating more power than the Bonneville Dam and flashing more fire than a four-alarm blaze."

HERE COMES THE SUN

Oregon's victory over SMU in the 1963 Sun Bowl came 46 years after the school's last postseason win in the 1917 Rose Bowl. The victory also avenged a defeat to the Mustangs in the 1949 Cotton Bowl, probably Oregon's biggest game between the two contests. But for Len Casanova's 1963 squad, the present would do just fine.

Just as they had against Oregon State, the Ducks spent the first half building a lead and the second half warding off comeback attempts. Oregon was again without Mel Renfro, whose hand injury a month earlier hadn't sufficiently healed. As ferociously talented as Renfro was, his absence meant Berry was throwing more. And coach Hayden Fry's SMU defense wasn't equipped to stop this NFL-bound passer.

H.D. Murphy's 49-yard interception set up Oregon's first touchdown, a Dennis Keller nine-yard run late in the first quarter. The Mustangs responded by driving to the Oregon three, but Murphy again picked off quarterback Danny Thomas. Seizing the momentum for good, Berry threw touchdown passes of 23 yards to Dick Imwalle and 20 yards to Paul Burleson. The second score came less than a minute before halftime after yet another Mustang turnover in Oregon territory. A scoreless third quarter made SMU's two late touchdowns mere window dressing on an Oregon victory.

Len Casanova would remain for three more years as coach, including another impressive campaign the next season at 7-2-1 behind Berry. But with Renfro and Dave Wilcox having played their last games in Eugene, the 1963 Sun Bowl marked the apex of Casanova's 16 seasons at Oregon and this magical early 1960s period for the Ducks.

"We had a lot of talent both offensively and defensively," Renfro reflects. "And Len Casanova, being a great coach, he really kept us on our toes. His pep talks were fiery and kept us going. What I remember most was that we played well together. There wasn't animosity or dissension or any problem children. We were all just out there working together to win."

THE KEYSTONE SLATE

The Ducks rattled off six straight victories to begin the 1964 season, which included two unlikely occurrences. First, Oregon's opening three games featured almost identical scores: 20-13, 22-13, and 22-14. And, in a non-conference scheduling anomaly, the Ducks faced Pittsburgh and Penn State in consecutive weeks. Both resulted in wins. One Penn State assistant that year was 38-year-old Joe Paterno, two seasons away from taking over the Nittany Lions' head job. The next time Oregon faced Paterno would be 30 years later in the 1995 Rose Bowl.

ONE POINT SHY OF ROSES

A blocked extra point was the difference between a Rose Bowl berth and no bowl at all for Len Casanova's 7-2-1 team in 1964.

Facing Oregon State in the second quarter of his last game in an Oregon uniform, quarterback Bob Berry marched his team 95 yards for an apparent tying touchdown on Dennis Keller's two-yard run. But after a bad snap, the Beavers' Al East blocked Oregon kicker Herm Meister's extra point attempt.

The Ducks had more than half the game to add to their lead, but despite 195 yards in passing, Berry and company couldn't generate any additional points. The 6-0 advantage held until the final minute, when Oregon State's Brooker Washington scored and Steve Jones' extra point put the host Beavers ahead for the first time before the final gun sounded.

Coach Tommy Prothro's team was headed for a Rose Bowl date with Michigan. Berry left Oregon as its most accomplished quarterback, but twice in three years as starter his teams missed Rose Bowl invitations after losing to Oregon State. Casanova would last two more years, both losing seasons, as coach.

For all these two men accomplished together at Oregon in three years, including winning an impressive 68 percent of the time, a Sun Bowl win, and All-America citations for Berry, just two Civil War plays—the pooch punt in 1962 and the blocked extra point in 1964—kept this legendary coach and quarterback from achieving much more.

UNTIL PALO ALTO

Three straight wins over Pittsburgh, Utah, and Brigham Young to begin 1965 vaulted the Berry-less Ducks to No. 10 in the United Press International coaches' poll. Oregon then lost a close 7-3 decision at Stanford that seemed to shatter the team's psyche. Replays confirmed that the Stanford player who scored the winning touchdown had stepped out of bounds illegally before making the catch.

A tie against Air Force and a 24-20 loss to Washington followed, then a narrow 17-14 win over Idaho, giving way to three more defeats, including a season-ending 19-14 loss to Oregon State. A team that had once been in the nation's top 10 now registered the Ducks' first losing campaign in four years. What's more, the 1964 Civil War was Oregon's second straight loss to OSU, part of a dismal eight-year losing streak to the Beavers.

CASANOVA'S LEGACY

By the time Len Casanova retired from coaching following the 1966 season, he had won 82 games and taken the team to four bowl contests

Head coach Len Casanova in a promotional shot from early in his tenure.
Image courtesy of Special Collections and University Archives, University of Oregon libraries

in a time when postseason play was far less prevalent. He had also led the Ducks to their first Rose Bowl since 1916. That day Oregon came within three points of upsetting the nation's No. 1 team. Legendary players like George Shaw, Mel Renfro, and Bob Berry flourished under Casanova, while he also mentored future coaching legends like John McKay and John Robinson.

Casanova's greatest contribution to the University of Oregon and its football team, however, was his influence on the hundreds of young men, helping to shape them as citizens, as leaders, and as people of character.

"Cas helped so many countless people who weren't necessarily great football players get through school and life," recalls Claxton Welch, a sophomore running back during Casanova's last season in 1966. "His staff was concerned about me not just as an athlete, but a person."

Welch remembers when, years after he graduated from Oregon and finished his NFL career, he happened to tell Casanova he'd moved to Los Angeles. "Cas gave me the names of all these prominent alumni down there. One guy I went to visit on the top floor of the Transamerica building. This larger-than-life man comes out in a $1,000 suit and introduces himself. He was the company president. He said, 'We have a lot of different companies, so whatever company you have an interest in going to work for, we can help you.' There were probably eight or 10 other alumni I met through Cas. That didn't have anything to do with playing on a winning team. That had to do with helping people."

Both as coach and athletic director, Casanova also helped Oregon steer clear of some of the racial and political tensions that were beginning to plague other schools and teams. In the late 1960s, for example, the Oregon State team was divided over a confrontation between head coach Dee Andros and linebacker Fred Milton, who refused Andros' order to shave his goatee. African-American players walked out, and OSU students even demonstrated. Andros shied away from recruiting blacks, and a football program at the height of its success gave way to more than a quarter-century of consecutive losing seasons. At Oregon, meanwhile, Casanova was helping African Americans find housing in Eugene when landlords turned them away.

Casanova was a man of strong Catholic faith, but he also walked a difficult line with players. Often those players that he knew came from religious homes were given wake-up calls on Sunday mornings for church. John Harrington, who was a member of Casanova's last recruiting class in 1966 and father of future Oregon star Joey Harrington, remembers the Oregon coach giving his mother rosary beads on a recruiting visit to the Harrington household. "He apparently had made some trip to Rome and got them at the Vatican," Harrington remembers with a chuckle. "He told us that they were blessed by the Pope. I had been vacillating between Washington, Washington State, and Oregon. But the minute that he gave those rosary beads to my mother I knew where I was going."

Yet Cas also understood when not to proselytize. More than anything, he led by example and formed individual bonds with players, coaches, and the greater Oregon family. Years after John Harrington graduated and became a head coach at Gresham, Oregon's Barlow High School in 1975, Casanova sent him a letter. "One piece of advice stuck with me that I've used as advice for other young coaches I've come in contact with since," Harrington recalls. "He said, 'You cannot treat every player the same, because no two people are the same.' I think what Cas was telling me, which I later came to understand, is that you have to have rules and expectations, but you cannot have so many rules that you botch yourself into a corner as a coach. You realize that sometimes a kid needs an arm around the shoulder. And other kids don't need that—they need a kick in the rear. I think that's what he was telling me, and I never forgot that."

In nearly everything he did, Casanova was a charmer, as popular with players' mothers as he was with the young men he coached. "I remember we were taking the train down to Berkeley for a game against heavily favored Cal," recalls John Gram, a student manager for the team in 1951. "My mother was making the trip, too, and about 10 o'clock at night we ran into Cas down in the bar car. She said, 'Mr. Casanova, do you really think you can win this game tomorrow?' I was so embarrassed. But Cas just looked at my mom, smiled and said, 'Ma'am, that's why we play the game.'" Oregon did indeed lose that game, but only by one point: 28-27.

On the score sheet, Casanova's final years at Oregon—both as coach and athletic director—came with more defeats than victories. But that never changed his reputation in the minds of all who knew him. If Bear Bryant remains the soul of Alabama, Woody Hayes the spirit of Ohio State, then Casanova remains at the heart of Oregon Ducks football.

3

TURBULENT TIMES
1967-1977

BUILDING AUTZEN STADIUM

BY THE LATE 1950s it was becoming clear that the 20,000-seat Hayward Field could not continue forever as the Duck football team's home. Oregon had long played many of its most significant games in Portland's Multnomah Stadium to accommodate large crowds, despite the fact that it was more than 100 miles from Eugene. They needed a bigger home...at home.

In 1960, the university purchased about 88 acres of land across the Willamette River from campus. Planning, design, and construction ensued over the next seven years. The architect was Skidmore, Owings, and Merrill (SOM), an internationally acclaimed firm that had designed numerous landmarks throughout the country, including Memorial Coliseum in Portland as well as Lever House in New York and, later, the Sears Tower in Chicago.

There are two principal design templates for larger sports stadiums: those with a series of upper decks and those with a single-level bowl shape. The latter design is more rare, but its sight lines are superb and its look a more elegant one, seen in the Rose Bowl and Michigan Stadium. SOM chose a bowl-shaped design for Oregon's new stadium, which was named for the project's largest donor, lumberman Thomas

J. Autzen. To minimize the impact of its size upon the surrounding landscape of single-story buildings, SOM built Autzen into the ground, with an outer rim landscaped in grass and a gently curving entry lane. Budget for the project was only about $2.5 million.

"I remember we used to take recruits there to this big pile of dirt," says Claxton Welch of Autzen's construction in 1966. "There were dump trucks going by one after the other and we'd say to the recruits, 'You have to visualize it. You have to dream.' But we had no idea of what it would be today."

The beginning of the Autzen era also marked the end of Len Casanova's tenure as head coach. Following two straight losing seasons, fans were restless, and after 16 seasons on the Oregon sidelines, Casanova was ready to retire from coaching. Two months after the 1966 season ended, he was named athletic director. Casanova's first action was to name offensive line coach Jerry Frei as the new head coach. "After my dad got hired, our whole family used to go out to the Autzen construction site on Sundays and hang out," remembers Terry Frei, Jerry's son and now a veteran sportswriter.

The stadium opened on September 23, 1967, to a crowd of 27,500 for Oregon's matchup with Colorado. The game was telecast nationwide by ABC, but the network was experiencing a strike at the time, so regular announcer Keith Jackson was replaced by Casanova and Colorado athletic director Dallas Ward. Credit for the first touchdown went to the Buffaloes' Bob Anderson. Oregon's first points in their new home were scored on a 26-yard touchdown reception by Denny Schuler, who would go on to be an assistant coach at his alma mater in the 1980s under Rich Brooks.

Colorado won the game that day 17-13. Oregon's first victory at Autzen wouldn't come for nearly a month, when quarterback John Harrington led the Ducks to a 31-6 rout over Idaho with two touchdown passes.

Over the ensuing decades, though, Autzen Stadium would eventually become known as one of the most difficult places in all of college football for opposing teams to play. In recent years, as the stadium has expanded and sellouts have become regular amidst the team's perennial winning seasons. Autzen has routinely appeared in media rankings of college football's best stadiums.

OREGON GETS FREI'D

When the Ducks moved into their new home at Autzen Stadium for the 1967 season, Oregon was playing with a new head coach for the first time since 1951 as offensive line coach Jerry Frei took over for Len Casanova.

A former World War II reconnaissance pilot in the Pacific who also played at Wisconsin with the great Elroy "Crazy Legs" Hirsch, Frei was a good man thrust into difficult circumstances. Casanova remained a legend, but the team had suffered two consecutive losing seasons before Frei took over. Despite the optimism of a new stadium, the team Frei inherited was low on talent and momentum.

The new coach had visited Notre Dame in the off-season and wanted to instill its traditions of team discipline and community support. He coined Oregon's "Fighting Ducks" moniker after the Fighting Irish, and initiated a pep rally in downtown Eugene the day before a game.

"We went around town riding on a fire engine," Welch recalls. "The rally squad was waiting for us downtown, but there was hardly anyone even on the street. Even when we got back to where we were having a bonfire, there were only about 20 people out there. But Jerry Frei saw the potential of turning Oregon into a real power. I think that's why Cas picked Jerry."

Frei was also an excellent recruiter, as he'd shown in the ensuing years by landing such stars as Bobby Moore and Dan Fouts. But as Oregon began its season in 1967, those days were still ahead. The team won only twice while both Welch and quarterback Tom Blanchard succumbed to knee injuries, Blanchard's serious enough to require a redshirt the next season. Oregon put up a valiant fight against No. 8-

ranked Oregon State and quarterback Steve Preece to conclude the year, but lost 14-10.

Amidst the assassinations of Martin Luther King and Robert Kennedy, 1968 brought another losing campaign, but there was reason for optimism since Frei seemed to have Oregon headed in the right direction. Had Blanchard been healthy, the 4-6 record could have easily been a winning one. The team lost three straight to begin the season, but there was no shame in going down against Stanford and future Heisman Trophy winner Jim Plunkett or losing on the road versus Ohio State.

While few believed in an Oregon team that had lost 11 of 13 in Frei's season and a half, the Ducks proceeded to surprise even supporters by winning three of their next four. And none were more satisfying than a narrow 3-0 defeat over Washington in Seattle. Frei had experimented with a few different quarterbacks in Blanchard's absence, including Eric Olson and Alan Pitcaithley. But sophomore John Harrington of Portland's Central Catholic High School got the start. Harrington didn't set the world on fire, but he drove Oregon to a 38-yard field goal by Seattle native Ken Woody (a future Ducks broadcaster) that won the game.

"Our defense kept us in a lot of games," Welch says. All-American Jim Smith, Omri Hildreth (who would die tragically in 1976), and future Kansas City Chiefs head coach Gunther Cunningham led the squad.

Oregon's most impressive game in 1968 was arguably a loss to USC. Trojans head coach John McKay returned to his alma mater with a No. 1 ranking and running back sensation O.J. Simpson, who would win the Heisman Trophy that year by the widest voting margin ever. But Frei's team held "The Juice" to 67 yards on 25 carries and outgained Southern California 152-87 on the ground. It was the second straight

Head coach Jerry Frei.
Image courtesy of Special Collections and University Archives, University of Oregon libraries

season that Oregon's defense held Simpson to far under his average. "I think I'll stay away from Oregon from now on," said the USC back, who would go on to even greater fame in the NFL and, years later, infamy in a murder trial that gripped the nation. "Oregon just doesn't like me."

HELP IS ON THE WAY

After back-to-back losing seasons, coach Jerry Frei and his staff began to benefit from a pack of talented new recruits. Offensive lineman Tom Drougas would achieve All-America status, as would receiver Bob Newland, who would also finish his career in Eugene as the school's most prolific pass catcher. But the biggest recruiting coup of Frei's first two years was a big, fast tailback from Tacoma named Bobby Moore.

As Vietnam War protests and tense racial politics came to dominate the Eugene campus during the late 1960s, enormous controversy could erupt on a college football team merely over the length of a player's hair. In particular, African Americans who favored Afro haircuts or beards faced conservative coaches eager to send them to a barber or the bench. Other schools would recruit several black players at the same position, so there would never be too many on the field at the same time. Schools with better records or more prestigious traditions sought the highly touted Moore, who would later change his name to Ahmad Rashad, but Oregon got the nod in part because Frei's staff was more progressive.

"A lot of people were shocked," Rashad recalls of his decision to play in Eugene. "It came down to Notre Dame and Oregon. With Notre Dame I was skeptical, because they had never had a black running back. I was afraid they were going to put me at defensive back. They kept promising me, 'You're going to be our first black running back.' But sometimes that never pans out. I knew Jerry Frei was an honest man, though."

The late 1960s and early 1970s were tumultuous on just about every college campus, but especially Oregon, where Vietnam protests happened almost daily. Between 1970 and '71 alone, two buildings, Johnson Hall and Campbell Hall, were bombed, and two more, the ROTC building and Esslinger Hall, were damaged by fire. Most football programs insulated their players as much as possible from the revolutionary times, housing them together in player-only dorms and discouraging any political activity. But Moore liked that Frei was more lenient. "Some guys would miss practice because they were at a protest, and that was okay," Rashad remembers. "That never happened anywhere else."

Oregon's slow but steady trajectory toward respectability and a winning record continued throughout 1969. Quarterback Tom Blanchard was back from injury and connected with Moore early and often. The team was improved, but still faced as many downs as ups in a 5-5-1 season. A blowout 28-0 loss to Jim Plunkett's Stanford was followed by a one-point win over Washington State and a two-point upset loss to San Jose State. The lowest moment came a week later against Air Force, a humiliating 60-13 loss after which Frei suggested he should perhaps resign.

But the players responded to their coach, taking the blame for their performance. Playing his first season of college football, Moore was approaching Mel Renfro's single-season scoring record, although Pat Verutti was still gaining more yards. The Ducks put together their only back-to-back wins of the season with a 22-7 defeat of Washington in Eugene and a 58-14 decision against Idaho. Another frustratingly close Civil War loss, this time 10-7, featured an astonishing 24 unassisted tackles by Moore's fellow super sophomore, linebacker Tom Graham. OSU usually marks the regular season's end, but that year, Oregon was able to take out their Civil War frustrations the next week, pummeling Hawaii 57-16.

The Ducks were right at .500 for the season, and there was hope as the team relaxed beside Waikiki Beach. Finally healthy, Blanchard was coming back for his senior season, Moore was ready to explode, and a young quarterback named Dan Fouts was beginning to impress his coaches in practice. Fans would soon have the same impression.

FORMERLY KNOWN AS BOBBY MOORE

To sports fans who grew up in the '80s and '90s, he is Ahmad Rashad, the TV broadcaster covering football and basketball for NBC Sports. He famously proposed to *The Cosby Show* star Phylicia Ayers-Allen during pregame of a Thanksgiving Day broadcast in 1985. (She said yes.) Others a little older may recall Rashad as the four-time Pro Bowl Minnesota Vikings wide receiver in the late 1970s and early '80s. His game-winning Hail Mary reception to win the 1980 Central Division title became known as the "Miracle Catch." But first Rashad was Bobby Moore, a running back from Tacoma arguably as talented as any Oregon has ever produced. "He was just head and shoulders above everyone as a player," Dan Fouts says. "Even among us, his teammates, he was this star."

From his first game, Moore dazzled. In a 28-17 victory against Utah, Moore caught a school-record three touchdown passes from Blanchard. "It seemed to come easy to me that day," he remembers. "I was in a flow." That year, Moore broke Mel Renfro's single-season scoring record with 92 points on 15 touchdowns. Moore also tied the school's single-season reception record and led the Pacific-8 Conference in scoring.

In his junior season, which began a few weeks after the Apollo 11 moon landing, Moore was paired with future Pro Football Hall of Fame quarterback Dan Fouts for the first time. No one knew it then, but this marked the first occasion in which Oregon had two future Pro Bowl players in the same backfield. "Dan was just such a competitor," Rashad remembers. "He was a nice guy, but he had a lip on him. I remember hearing from teammates how they'd go out to some tavern to shoot

Running back and receiver Ahmad Rashad, then known as Bobby Moore.
Image courtesy of Special Collections and University Archives, University of Oregon libraries

pool and Dan and some logger would end up having to be pulled away from each other." That year Frei's team finished with its first winning record in six seasons as Moore, kept out of two games with injuries, ran for 924 yards to break Mel Renfro's single-season record by more than 150 yards.

As a senior, Moore was on fire, rushing for more than 100 yards on six occasions, including a 249-yard burst against Utah in which he also amassed 89 receiving yards and threw a 34-yard touchdown pass. He also rushed for 191 yards against Washington, 161 against WSU, and 150 against Stanford. Moore obliterated his own Oregon single-season rushing record with 1211 yard in 10 games, earning first-team All-America status.

Moore's career as a Duck didn't end the way he would have liked, though. Oregon finished a disappointing 5-6 in 1971, including a heartbreaking 30-29 Civil War loss in Moore's final game.

After changing his name to Ahmad Rashad in 1972 following his conversion to Islam, he was the NFL's fourth overall pick to the St. Louis Cardinals. In pre-draft prognostications that year, Rashad was not only named the top-skilled running back, but he was also listed as the draft's best wide receiver. But it was at first disillusioning for such an intelligent, charismatic young man to leave the protective environment of progressive Eugene.

"The worst year of my career was the year after I left Oregon for St. Louis," he says. "There were racial divisions there that we didn't have. I remember they even had two different prayer groups, one for black players and one for white players. I told them, 'You're both crazy.' It reminded me that at Oregon we had such a great camaraderie. I loved all the guys on my team. That never happens anymore in life. We always feel like nobody really looked up to us as a team. It was always about USC or UCLA or Stanford. But the little Ducks, we fought hard and we played hard. And we had guys who got the maximum out of their ability."

WATCH OUT FOR THE SKINNY SOPHOMORE

If football fans from outside the state of Oregon were to name the most famous former Duck football player, the majority would probably choose Dan Fouts. A Hall of Fame quarterback for the San Diego Chargers, Fouts finished his 14-year NFL career as one of only three players to pass for 40,000 yards. After his playing days, Fouts followed in his father's footsteps as an esteemed TV commentator and broadcaster for ABC, which he continues today. In fact, he's covered some of Oregon's most recent high-profile victories over Michigan in 2003 and Oklahoma in 2006.

Fouts wasn't highly recruited, but he played for a very good team, St. Ignatius in San Francisco. Assistant coach George Siefert, then in charge of Oregon's Bay Area recruiting, first noticed Fouts as a junior while recruiting offensive lineman Jim Figoni. When Oregon played against Stanford, Siefert brought head coach Jerry Frei and offensive coordinator John Robinson to see Fouts and Figoni compete. "I had a good game that day," he remembers, "and they remembered me come recruiting time the next year." Athletic director Len Casanova, who was a friend of his broadcaster father, also courted Fouts.

When Fouts arrived in Eugene as a freshman in the fall of 1969, he quarterbacked the freshman team to an 0-4 record under future Seattle Seahawks defensive coordinator John Marshall. Although Fouts became eligible for varsity as a sophomore, Jerry Frei already had a starting quarterback, Tom Blanchard, on his team. And most of the attention devoted to younger recruits was going to Fouts' teammate, Bobby Moore.

But in his first game as a sophomore in 1970, Fouts was called to action immediately after Blanchard was injured against Cal. No one else was more surprised than Fouts himself. "In our offensive meetings," he recalls, "the last thing John Robinson said was for everybody to be ready: 'Everybody in this room is going to play except one guy.' And he looked right at me and he said, 'Fouts is not going to play. The reason he's not going to play is Blanchard's going to play the whole game. He's our guy, he's our senior, and he's a great quarterback.' I think he said that to give Tom a boost, because Tom had been battling a knee injury his entire career. And actually, when he said that, I kind of felt relieved. I didn't want to play—I was just a stupid sophomore!"

Fouts entered the game with Oregon trailing and, inexperience aside, was expected to produce. "They put me in and Robinson called the bomb," he says. "I got in the huddle and I was so cotton-mouthed I don't know if anyone could hear me." Fouts actually threw a very good pass, but Bob Newland dropped it. By game's end, though, he rallied the Ducks to victory, 31-24, in Oregon's last appearance in Portland.

Fouts set a new Oregon record for interceptions with 24 that season, but he also threw for 2,390 yards along the way—the most ever by a Duck quarterback. Oregon enjoyed its first winning season in six years at 6-4-1. The next season's record was a disappointing 5-6, and Jerry Frei was fired afterward. But Fouts persevered under Dick Enright his senior year, despite a frustrating 4-7 campaign and an offensive system that didn't harness his skills. Luckily, an emphatic 30-3 victory over Oregon State, Fouts' first, sent him to the NFL on a winning note.

Fouts finished his career as Oregon's all-time leading passer with 5,995 yards, as well as touchdown passes (37) and total offense leader (5,871). Ultimately, he set 19 school records. Oregon never made it to a bowl game in the early 1970s with Fouts and Bobby Moore on campus, and after they left the team suffered its most downtrodden period in history. But that's all the more reason to look back on Dan Fouts' career at Oregon as one of greatness.

BOBBY, PRE, AND BOWERMAN

When Bobby Moore came to Oregon as its most highly touted recruit since Mel Renfro, another athletic celebrity was already on campus: legendary distance runner Steve Prefontaine. Big fish in a small pond, the two became fast friends.

"Pre was just the coolest guy," Ahmad Rashad remembers. "He wasn't like your typical cross-country runner: cerebral little skinny guy. He had a bulldog attitude. He'd have been a great football player just because of that. He partied a little harder than I did, but we hit it off right off the bat."

Moore also befriended Oregon track coach Bill Bowerman, who was making prototype running shoes—soon to be known as Nikes—with Phil Knight. "Bowerman didn't talk much," Rashad continues. "He was a tough guy, but he was warm, too. If he liked you, he really liked you. And if he didn't like you, he never had the time of day for you." Between Moore's freshman and sophomore years, he underwent a Bowerman-supervised running and conditioning program.

"He called me into his office and gave me these shoes he wanted me to wear while I ran," Rashad adds. "They were funny looking shoes. You could put them on either foot—there wasn't a left or a right. They were hand sewn with the sole glued onto the bottom. Bowerman told me, 'Go as far as you can, stop, and run back. And each day go a little bit further.' One day Pre ran with me. The funniest thing was, I had never done any jogging or anything like that, and I'm out there with this world-class runner. Pre was talking the whole time and I couldn't talk back because I was so tired. I went about a mile and came back. But he just kept running. Later I got in my car and I was driving home, and when I was about 10 miles from campus I saw him run by. He was still going."

UCLA? WE SEE A CLASSIC.

In 1970, Oregon had both the benefit and challenge of two good quarterbacks: senior Tom Blanchard and sophomore Dan Fouts. Blanchard was the starter but perennially injured. They combined to beat Cal. The next week at Illinois, Blanchard threw the longest pass play in Oregon football history, 95 yards, to Bob Newland. The Ducks lost 20-16, though, when Bobby Moore was stopped at the one-yard line with less than two minutes to play. In Fouts' first start against Rose Bowl bound Stanford and Heisman winner-to-be Jim Plunkett, Oregon lost 33-10. Still, after just three outings, Blanchard and Fouts had combined for the nation's top passing offense at 326 yards per game.

Then there is Oregon's legendary 41-40 comeback win in Los Angeles against UCLA. Fouts started and played almost the entire game, but with 4:28 remaining and his team trailing 40-21, he was knocked unconscious in the melee to recover a fumbled goal-line snap. "The ball had some moisture on it and my buddy Figoni snapped it between my legs," Fouts recalls of his high school and college center. "It never got to me. So I'm looking for it and I get hit right on top of the head and get knocked cold."

The hobbling Blanchard took over, driving Oregon to a 29-yard Bobby Moore touchdown in just three plays. UCLA fumbled on its ensuing drive, and this time Blanchard needed just two plays to find Moore for another touchdown. But Oregon was still down 40-35 with 2:24 remaining. That's when the special teams unit came through with an onside kick recovery by Don Frease.

Blanchard had separated his shoulder on a sweep play to Rashad, but tried to keep playing. "We used to do this kind of stupid thing on sweeps where we'd pitch the ball back to Ahmad and we were told as quarterbacks to act as pulling guards: get out and front and just roll at somebody's feet," Fouts remembers. "Tom did that and the whole pile came down on top of him." Blanchard even completed a long throw to Leland Glass to the five before coming out. "And as Leland's coming off the line of scrimmage he gets poked in the eye," Fouts adds. "So the ball is being thrown by a guy with a separated shoulder to a guy with one eye. It was just unbelievable."

Despite his probable concussion, Fouts replaced Blanchard at the five-yard line. On his first play, he was sacked for about a 10-yard loss. "Ken Woody [Oregon's kicker] was Glass' replacement," Fouts continues with a laugh. "I go back to pass and get chased out of the pocket looking for Woody. I can't find him because he's so short." Seconds later, though, Fouts connected over the middle with tight end

Greg Specht for a game-winning 15-yard touchdown. After the game, Jerry Frei wiped tears from his eyes while he met with reporters. Blanchard cried too—because the pain in his shoulder was so intense when he jumped up cheering after the winning score.

The win made Oregon 3-2. Two games later, the team would even climb into the Rose Bowl race after beating mighty USC 10-7 in Eugene for a 5-2 mark. But the euphoria was premature as Washington broke the Ducks' hearts 25-23 a week later. Next Oregon faced undefeated, No. 9-ranked Air Force without Bobby Moore, who was suspended for one game after an off-field arrest in Portland. Undeterred, Fouts passed the team to a 46-35 upset while fog enveloped Autzen. But Army then forced a tie, and Oregon State scored a 24-9 Civil War victory. "I was horrible in Corvallis that day—with a capital H," Fouts says. Nevertheless, at 6-4-1, Oregon had its only winning season in a 14-year period between 1965 and 1978.

WHAT ABOUT BOB

Oregon's MVP of the 1970 season was actually not Bobby Moore, Dan Fouts, or Tom Blanchard, but receiver Bob Newland. During his three years of play, Newland became Oregon's most prolific receiver ever with 125 receptions, 13 touchdowns, and 1,941 yards. As a senior versus Air Force in 1970, he tied the Oregon record for receptions with 11. Against Illinois, he caught the longest touchdown pass in school history, 95 yards from Blanchard, and earned a whopping 225 receiving yards—also a team best. Newland finished the season with 67 receptions and 1,123 yards (both records), along with an All-America selection. He was chosen in the seventh round of the NFL draft by New Orleans in 1971 and played five seasons.

WINN WINS

In 1971, the Ducks hit the road for Los Angeles to score one of their most unlikely victories. Dan Fouts was injured, and the mighty Trojans, coached by Oregon alum John McKay, were gearing up for national championships in two of the next three seasons.

Replacing Fouts in the lineup was 5-foot-8 Harvey Winn, who proceeded to do just that against stunned Southern California. With All-America offensive tackle Tom Drougas' protection and running back Bobby Moore's solid ground game (Moore would become Oregon's all-time leading rusher a week later), Winn completed 17 of 25 passes for three touchdowns. The Ducks trailed USC 23-14 in the fourth quarter, but scored two late touchdowns to go up 28-23 and hold on for the Winn.

VICTORY BY A FINGERNAIL

A week after Winn's USC heroics, the quarterback couldn't replicate the same effectiveness against Washington. He was replaced by Dan Fouts, who had a classic duel with Husky quarterback Sonny Sixkiller. Two other Oregon players saved the day. With Washington nursing a 21-16 lead, Duck defensive back Dave Piper intercepted Sixkiller for the go-ahead touchdown, holding out the ball and taunting the nearest Husky defender as he raced to the end zone.

Sixkiller came storming back, driving Washington for a game-winning field goal attempt at game's end. But Bill Drake, perhaps Oregon's best defensive back at the time, blocked the ball—just barely. The pigskin had ripped off his fingernail. "He came over to the sidelines holding up his middle digit with blood dripping down," Fouts says, "and celebrating like crazy."

GOODBYE FREI, HELLO LOSING

At the end of the 1971 season, all signs appeared that Jerry Frei would continue as head coach. The team's 5-6 record was disappointing given talent like Fouts and Moore, the latter of whom was

Quarterback Dan Fouts hands off to Ahmad Rashad (Bobby Moore) in 1970. *Image courtesy of Special Collections and University Archives, University of Oregon libraries*

surprisingly kept out of a heartbreaking 30-29 Civil War loss (his last collegiate game) at season's end with a bruised left leg. But Dan Fouts was about to return for his senior season, and reason for optimism remained. After the holidays Frei had even coached in the Hula Bowl all-star game alongside national champion Nebraska's Bill Devaney.

Yet pressure was building from alumni, mostly in Portland, for action to be taken after the losing season and, most importantly, Frei's now 0-5 Civil War record. After assistant coaches John Robinson and Norm Chapman left the team (Robinson for a USC assistant coach position, Chapman to retire from football), it was suggested that Frei should wipe the slate clean with an entirely new staff, firing his remaining assistants. One was George Siefert, who would later win two Super Bowls as the head coach of Joe Montana- and Steve Young-led San Francisco 49er teams. Frei, still grieving over the recent death of his father, refused to let Siefert and the remaining staff go. Instead, he promptly resigned on January 19, 1972.

"It was gutless leadership on the part of the administration," Fouts says. "They didn't recognize what they had. And as players, we were pissed." Then, instead of searching for a bright young coaching mind or an experienced veteran coach, the school hired defensive line coach Dick Enright, who had joined the team in 1970 after his playing career with the Los Angeles Rams was cut short by an auto accident. "I was on that quote-unquote search committee," Fouts adds. "He wasn't anywhere near qualified. He had only been a coach for one year. I mean, hello?"

His players and coaches—including the legendary Len Casanova, who hired him—agreed that Jerry Frei was a man of tremendous character. "He was a father-like figure," Ahmad Rashad recalls. "His role was that he'd turn a young kid into a man. That was what he thought a football coach did. He would try to win football games, and he wanted the best players to come there. But more importantly, by the time you left Oregon he wanted you to become a responsible human being involved in a lot of different things."

The success of his recruits at Oregon and later in the NFL, as well as consecutively better records in each of his first four seasons, showed that Frei could build a winning program. But college football was increasingly becoming a high-stakes, win-at-all-costs business, and coaches were being fired for fewer losses than Frei had posted.

Still, Frei's firing clearly hurt the Oregon program. From 1972-1978, the Ducks suffered seven straight losing seasons and would see two more head coaches fired before Rich Brooks finally brought stability and winning back to Eugene. Just as America's executive branch began to implode in the early 1970s amidst the Watergate scandal, so too was the Oregon football program humbled and in need of leadership.

FOUTS FINALÉ BESTS BEAVERS

Another up-and-down season in Eugene came in 1972. Oregon was overmatched against powerhouses Oklahoma and national champion-to-be USC, then suffered frustratingly close losses to Missouri and Washington. Dick Enright had Fouts to throw the ball and a future NFL Pro Bowl tight end in Russ Francis to catch it. Instead, Enright wanted his drop-back passer to run the option. "I just thought, 'What's going on here?'" Fouts says. Despite what was arguably an improved defense, the Ducks had just three victories going into the annual season's-end contest with Oregon State.

Oregon finished with a fourth win, though, and a particularly satisfying one. The Beavers had won eight straight Civil Wars, but this time they never stood a chance. On the first play from scrimmage, tailback Don Reynolds ran for a 60-yard touchdown, and the Ducks never looked back. Later in the first half, Fouts hit Greg Lindsey on a 65-yard touchdown and Tim Guy blocked and recovered an OSU punt in the end zone. Oregon obliterated Dee Andros' team, leading 27-3 at halftime before coasting to a 30-3 win. And it could have been even more of a blowout: after Fouts exited in the fourth quarter (soon to be seen on the sideline with a cigar), backup Norval Turner drove the Ducks to the Beaver one-yard line but ran out the clock without scoring. "We had some big wins when I was at Oregon—memorable wins," Fouts says. "But beating the Beavers in the last game I ever played as a Duck is right at the top of the list."

At game's end, things got ugly. Before time had even expired, Oregon fans tore down the Parker Stadium goal post and even started charging Oregon State players with a piece of it until predictable fisticuffs ensued.

The breakthrough win also brought memories of Oregon's fired coach, who had been sacrificed largely because of his 0-5 Civil War record. "I wish Jerry Frei were here," Enright told *The Oregonian*. "Even if he was head coach. This was for Frei. My heart was with him and his was with us. He got most of these guys here and he's still part of the team."

SUPER MARIO

For decades tradition had dictated at virtually all schools that incoming freshmen didn't play varsity football. But from the time he first laced up his cleats as an incoming 18-year-old in the fall of 1972, Mario Clark was too talented to keep off the Autzen Stadium field. He earned conference player of the week honors that first season and was a solid presence at cornerback on Dick Enright's 4-7 team. By the time he was a senior in 1975, Clark had accumulated 13 interceptions and was named both first-team all-conference and defensive player of the game in the Senior Bowl all-star game. A first-round selection by the Buffalo Bills, Clark was All-Rookie in 1976 and went on to win a Super Bowl with the San Francisco 49ers nine years (and 26 interceptions) later.

A 58-0 REPRIEVE

On October 27, 1973, en route to a miserable 2-9 record under second-year coach Dick Enright, the Ducks pasted a 58-0 victory on Washington.

For the first three games that season, Enright had started Norv Turner at quarterback. Turner would go on to greater notoriety as a successful NFL offensive coordinator and coach, winning two Super Bowls under Jimmy Johnson's Dallas Cowboys in the early 1990s before becoming head man for the Washington Redskins, Oakland Raiders, and San Diego Chargers. But with Turner under center in 1973, the Ducks started 1-5 and Enright supplanted Turner with Herb Singleton, only Oregon's second African-American starting quarterback. Against Washington, Singleton was on fire, throwing three touchdown passes.

This was a rare down year for Washington, which like Oregon had only one win going into the game. For Enright and company, it was a moment to savor in an otherwise gloomy season. The team would not win another game.

ENRIGHT'S EXIT

Five weeks after 1973's season-ending 17-14 Civil War loss to Oregon State, Enright was fired on January 4 with two years remaining on his contract. He was replaced by assistant Don Read. Going 6-16 was certainly grounds for termination in the increasingly high-stakes game of college football, not to mention the strategy behind it.

"In 1972, Dick Enright had one of the greatest passers in football history," Ahmad Rashad says, "and he made Dan Fouts an option quarterback for his senior year. I mean, what else do you have to say?"

Still, there may have been other reasons related to Enright's firing. "He became extremely religious," says John Gram, who was president of the Oregon Club of Portland that year and had been a student manager for both Jim Aiken and Len Casanova. "Dick Enright alienated a lot of folks, saying they had to pray."

Over the next few seasons, though, a prayer is what Oregon too often didn't have, as the team continued a mid-1970s downward spiral.

ONE SEASON AS SPRINGBOARD

If Mario Clark got off to an unprecedented fast start at Oregon, Russ Francis did just the opposite. Francis broke his leg in 1972 and was out most of the season, missing the chance to play with Dan Fouts. But in 1973, people were suddenly talking about the young tight end. Against Air Force, Oregon lost a tough 24-17 contest, but Francis helped keep the Ducks in the game with a dramatic 68-yard touchdown pass from Norv Turner. That season he'd catch 31 passes for 495 yards, good enough for All-Pac 10 honors and a first-round selection to New England in the NFL draft. It was as a professional that Francis really made his name, with four Pro Bowl selections and, like his former teammate Clark, a Super Bowl ring with San Francisco in 1985.

REYNOLDS RAPTURE

Oregon has often featured small but exceptionally talented players, particularly running backs, who combined dazzling speed and agility with an extra hunger to prove themselves after so often being underestimated. The performances of one such player, tailback Don Reynolds, gave fans rare moments of excitement during Oregon's lean years.

Reynolds didn't play much as a sophomore in 1972, but he averaged an astonishing 8.1 yards per carry, including an 85-yard run against Stanford that remains Oregon's second-longest run from scrimmage.

As a junior in 1973, Reynolds became only the second Duck player to surpass the 1,000-yard mark for the season. Against Utah he gained 290 all-purpose yards, and later racked up 178 on the ground versus Cal. His 46-yard touchdown in a nationally televised game against Air Force may have been the most memorable. A precursor of Barry Sanders, Reynolds changed direction numerous times as he zigzagged in and out of Falcon defenders. As a senior, his best game came against Northwestern, when Reynolds gained 196 yards on 23 carries for an 8.5-yard average. By graduation, No. 22 was second only to Ahmad Rashad in total yards at Oregon and only the second Duck, following Mel Renfro, to lead the team in rushing three straight years.

BLOWOUTS

To witness just how low the Oregon football program had fallen by the mid-1970s, look no further than two consecutive opening-day games with almost identical scores. On September 14, 1974, coach Don Read's team traveled to Lincoln, Nebraska, for a 61-7 shellacking by the Cornhuskers. And 364 days later, they began the 1975 season with a 62-7 humiliation at Oklahoma.

These weren't the only blowouts the Ducks endured. Against Washington in '74, Oregon lost 66-0. Facing UCLA a year later, the score was 50-17. In 1976, USC whipped the Ducks 53-0 before the Bruins defeated the team 46-0.

Of course it's not fair to judge coach Don Read's three-year tenure only by its worst moments. After all, Read posted an improved record each season: 2-9, 3-8, and 4-7. And when the now legendary Rich Brooks replaced Read in 1977, the team initially regressed in comparison, winning only four times in Brooks' first two seasons.

Amidst meager facilities and low budgets, the three men who led Oregon in the decade between 1967 and '76 collectively produced just one winning team, in 1970 under Frei. Just as America was celebrating its Bicentennial in 1976, Oregon was mired in the depths of despair.

4

BROOKS THE MAVERICK
1977-1988

A BEAVER AS COACH? THAT'S RICH.

BY THE TIME OREGON HIRED RICH BROOKS as coach just before Christmas in 1976, the program was at a low point in its history. After unsuccessfully courting future NFL head coaches Bill Walsh and Jim Mora, the school was preparing to sign an alumnus of archrival Oregon State. In fact, it was Brooks' famous pooch-punt in 1962 that helped set in motion a Terry Baker-led comeback win and kept Len Casanova's team out of a bowl game. Hiring Brooks, it seemed, would either be the final nail in Oregon's coffin or a stroke of genius.

Once an assistant under Dick Nolan with the San Francisco 49ers and Terry Donahue at UCLA, the 35-year-old Brooks was eager for his first try at a head coaching job—something he had narrowly missed the year before after interviewing at his alma mater. In the years ahead, Brooks would make the Beavers rue the day they denied him, compiling an unprecedented 14-3-1 Civil War record against his former team.

Brooks wasn't an overnight success at Oregon. There were early triumphs at the close of the 1970s, then years of losing again after the team was put on probation. But from the mid-1980s onward, Rich Brooks led the Ducks on a steady climb out of the quicksand. When

Oregon finally won its first outright Pac-10 championship in 1994, the children born when Brooks was hired back in 1976 had become high school seniors. There's a reason the playing surface at Autzen Stadium is now called Rich Brooks Field. By the time he left Eugene for the NFL shortly after the 1995 Rose Bowl, this one-time enemy Beaver combatant had become the Ducks' savior.

But in December 1976, that day remained almost 19 years away. As the presidency changed hands from Gerald Ford to Jimmy Carter, Oregon wasn't looking for a Rose Bowl so much as some stability. "He was a man well suited for that particular time in Oregon football," says Neal Zoumboukos, an assistant under Brooks and Mike Bellotti, "simply because the program needed a firm hand. He provided that."

Brooks brought an ideal balance to the job. With a gruff, no-nonsense personality, the head coach radiated a control that belied his young age. At the same time, Brooks was smart enough to trust the people around him.

"He was a person who delegated responsibility," Zoumboukos adds. "He was not a micromanager in any way, shape, or form. But he expected results. If you didn't get it done, you heard about it. Even though he had a so-called hard exterior, he listened very well to his players and to his coaches. You just kind of had to get past that exterior sometimes, but the man truly cared. And I think in time all of his players came to realize—when they were through playing or shortly thereafter—just how much he did care for them."

SETTLING IN, BUT NOT SETTLING

When Brooks took command of the Oregon program, a renewed optimism existed in Eugene—but it didn't last long. The Ducks wound up finishing 2-9 in both 1977 and 1978.

Part of the problem was scheduling. With a low athletic department budget, Oregon continually played non-conference road games against

Head coach Rich Brooks. *Image provided by John Giustina*

top opponents. In 1977, Brooks' team played respectably at Georgia in a 27-16 loss, but was throttled by Louisiana State 56-17. Then there were the usual Trojans, Huskies, and Bruins, who collectively outscored Oregon 108-18 that year.

Luckily there was one saving grace on the Duck schedule: the OSU Beavers, who were even worse than Oregon. In 1977, the green and gold took out their frustrations on Brooks' old team, 28-16. "Oregon, a team stung by big plays all season, came up with a variety of its own this afternoon," reported *The Oregonian*'s Dwayne Hartnett.

With nothing to lose, Brooks coached fearlessly. Oregon's first touchdown, a one-yard run by fullback Kim Nattung less than three minutes into the game, was set up by a 66-yard halfback pass from freshman Gary Beck to split end Ken Page. The second touchdown came after a fake field goal on fourth down at the OSU six-yard line. Oregon scored three touchdowns in the second quarter alone and led 28-10 at halftime, coasting the rest of the way for a victory. By game's end, the first-year coach of a 2-9 team was carried off the Autzen Stadium field on his players' shoulders.

The identical record in 1978 belied the team's improvement. Brooks, like Jerry Frei, hit the recruiting trail hard to turn around the team, landing key defenders like Vince Goldsmith, Mike Nolan, and Brian Hinkle, as well as offensive standouts like running back Vince Williams. Although a loss is a loss, Oregon was competitive, losing by three points to Wisconsin, one to Brigham Young, and two to UCLA. An underdog in the Civil War, Oregon won 24-3. And it wasn't a fluke: Brooks' team had momentum, and after eight straight losing seasons the Ducks were headed back into the winning ranks.

FIRED UP

In 1979 and '80, amidst the Iran hostage crisis and Three Mile Island nuclear disaster, Rich Brooks seemed to have Oregon transformed with consecutive winning seasons. In hindsight, knowing the Ducks would follow with three straight losing campaigns from 1981-1983, these two seasons were a brief reprieve.

The key to Oregon's success was dual-threat quarterback Reggie Ogburn. A junior college transfer, his first game in 1979 was on the road against a heavily favored Colorado team coached by Chuck Fairbanks, who had just come from the New England Patriots. The matchup also became the first live football contest broadcast by new sports cable network ESPN. Ogburn ran for 108 yards and passed for 168 as the Ducks upset the Buffaloes 33-19. "They just didn't know what to do with him," Brooks remembers.

The rest of the season would be an up-and-down affair, the Colorado win followed by three straight losses to Michigan State, Washington, and Purdue. Ogburn and company went 5-2 after that, however, with a 24-3 Civil War victory, giving Oregon its first winning season since 1970 and its first under Brooks.

"Fire Up" was 1980's marketing slogan, and the team was eager to continue the positive momentum. After six games in an era before overtime, though, Oregon found itself with the unusual record of 2-2-2. One of those ties was to a heavily favored USC team, though, and the wins had been convincing ones: 35-7 over Michigan State and 34-10 over the Huskies, Washington's only conference loss in a Rose Bowl campaign. From there, Oregon rattled off four straight victories, including a 40-21 hammering of Oregon State in a sunny but frigid Civil War in which Ogburn ran for 173 yards—the most ever by an Oregon quarterback—on just 14 carries.

Oregon finished 6-3-2 in 1980 with a seemingly bright future. But the Ducks would garner a winning record in only one of their next six seasons.

STRIKING GOLDSMITH

Defensive tackle Vince Goldsmith was a constant and menacing presence for Oregon in the late 1970s. Part of Rich Brooks' first recruiting class in 1977, Goldsmith made 13 tackles in his college debut during a tough road game against Georgia. But his most productive year was as a sophomore when he made 87 tackles, 62 of which were unassisted.

Goldsmith twice earned first-team all-conference honors while becoming Oregon's first defensive player to receive the Morris Trophy as the nation's top lineman. (Haloti Ngata would later match that feat.) A 1980 second-team All-American as a senior, he finished his collegiate career with 281 tackles. Although small for the NFL at 5-foot-11, Goldsmith played 10 years in the Canadian Football League, where his career total of 130.5 sacks is fifth best in league history. He was inducted into the University of Oregon Hall of Fame in 1982.

PROBATION BLUES

Before the 1980 season began, Oregon, along with four other Pac-10 schools, was implicated in a scandal in which athletes were given phony credits for classes they never took at a California junior college. Oregon was also charged specifically for illegal travel reimbursement for players. Offensive coordinator John Becker resigned, Brooks and five remaining assistants were fined, and several players were ruled ineligible. The school was stripped of three scholarships and disqualified from postseason play in 1980. Oregon had finally returned to winning ways under Brooks only to lose precious confidence and momentum. The coach offered his resignation, but then-UO president William Boyd turned it down. "We have conducted as thorough an investigation as I know how," he said in 1980. "I still find Rich Brooks an honorable coach."

The probation's impact may not have been immediate, as star quarterback Reggie Ogburn led the team to a second straight winning season in 1980. (1979-1980 had been Oregon's first back-to-back victorious seasons since 1963-1964.) But it's no coincidence that the team collapsed on the field in 1981 and '82 with just two wins in each season, falling like the Dow-Jones average amidst an early Ronald Reagan-era recession. Certainly Brooks' team was hurt by the loss of senior talent and leadership, especially Ogburn's, which contributed to the frustration of these years. But football programs can blossom or decay largely on reputation, and the sense of an up-and-coming Pac-10 team with a bright young coach gave way to clouds of uncertainty.

With a humbled but resilient Brooks leading the way, Oregon dusted itself off and again began the climb to respectability. It would take a few years before the team matched its success of 1979 and '80, but as the decade continued and the wins progressively mounted, Boyd's validation of Brooks would pay dividends.

PART SKILL, PART LUCK

When Notre Dame came to Autzen Stadium in 1982, it was the first time one of college football's legendary teams (other than fellow Pac-10 teams like USC) had done so. But this wasn't exactly a glorious clash of titans. Oregon was 0-6 going into the game, having already lost to John Robinson's Trojans by more than four touchdowns and embarrassed 10-4 at home against Fresno State. And in the early '80s, Fighting Irish teams of former high school coach Gerry Faust were a far cry from the heroics of past Notre Dame teams helmed by Knute Rockne and Ara Parseghian.

Still, it was more than a little exciting for Duck fans when Terrance Jones' one-yard touchdown in the fourth quarter gave Oregon a 13-10 lead. Despite the team's dismal 2-8-1 record in 1982, Rich Brooks' team boasted a stingy defense led by seniors like Mike Walter and Greg Mosure. But in the final minute, the Irish suddenly discovered an offense that had been grounded most of the day and marched down to the Oregon 18. Instead of going for the win, though, Notre Dame's coach chose to kick a field goal for the tie. It was a moral victory for the Ducks, while for the Irish coach, accepting mediocrity was a tragedy of Faustian proportions.

ONE GOOD PASS

Going into the 1982 Civil War, Oregon had only a single win to show for the entire season, and that had just come against Arizona the week before. In that game, the defense racked up five interceptions. Another gallant effort would be needed against OSU. The Beavers were held to just six points for the game, but it was nearly enough to give much maligned coach Joe Avezzano's winless squad the victory.

Oregon sophomore quarterback Mike Jorgensen possessed an excellent command of the field and, given proper protection, could pass well. (He's since become a longtime color commentator for Ducks radio broadcasts.) And despite the losses, Brooks' team remained close and liked to have fun, playing perhaps the best-known practical joke in team history.

"We wrapped poor Mike around the goal post with tape, poured maple syrup over his head, and I cut open a down coat for some feathers," defensive lineman Mike Walter recalls with a laugh. "I still remember poor Mike going, 'Okay guys. Okay. This isn't funny anymore.'" After Walter graduated and began playing for the Dallas Cowboys a few years later, he bought "a Danny White bobble-head doll, painted it green and yellow, glued a few feathers, and sent it to Mike. He's told me he's still got it displayed in his house."

Trailing the Beavers 6-0 in the final moments at rainy Parker Stadium, Jorgensen drove Oregon into Beaver territory. Needing only one touchdown to win, Jorgensen lofted the ball into the end zone and receiver Osborn Thomas snatched it up.

Eighteen years before 1982's Civil War game, Oregon State's 7-6 victory had kept the Ducks from going to the Rose Bowl. This time only pride was at stake, and even that seemed to be elusive for these two Pac-10 cellar dwellers. But this time the final score was 7-6 Oregon, and though it came with no fanfare, it marked the end of the Ducks' darkest days. There would be losing seasons after this, but only occasionally. From this moment, Rich Brooks' team was again on the rise.

HOUSTON, YOU HAVE A PROBLEM

Oregon's 15-14 victory over Houston in 1983 illustrated not only the steady progress Rich Brooks was making with the program, but also what a gambler the coach could be.

The Ducks were coming off consecutive two-win seasons, and patience was starting to thin as the team began 1983 with two losses (although, in all fairness, one was at Ohio State). Instead of giving his team a rest during the bye week before playing Houston, Brooks began holding two practices a day—something almost unheard of during the regular season. "I think Rich's actions heading into that game were more important than the game itself," assistant coach Steve Greatwood told *The Register-Guard*. "I'll never forget that week as a very young coach, going, 'He can't do that, can he?' And, 'By God, he is.'"

Houston had the nation's top-ranked rushing attack coming off its fifth bowl appearance in seven seasons. But Oregon was ready—and resilient. After the Cougars took a 7-0 lead in the final minutes of the first half, Ducks quarterback Mike Jorgensen lobbed a 53-yard touchdown pass to flanker Lew Barnes. But Brooks wasn't satisfied with tying the score. Oregon faked the extra-point attempt and holder Mike Owens passed to running back Alex Mack in the end zone, but Mack dropped the ball.

In the fourth quarter, Houston led 14-9 and appeared headed for more as the team drove inside the Ducks' 17. But on a crucial fourth-down play, linebacker Don Pellum threw rusher Donald Jordan for a loss on the option pitch. Needing to score, Oregon's offense fizzled out, facing fourth down on its own 39. But Brooks called for the second fake kick of the game, this time on a punt. Needing three yards, up-back Ladaria Johnson took a direct snap from the center and raced 17 yards for a first down in Houston territory.

Jorgensen found Barnes at the 25 for another first down, but Barnes fumbled and both teams scrambled for the ball. First Ducks rusher Kevin McCall reached it, but his momentum was too strong and the ball continued rolling toward the goal line. But mercifully for Oregon, tight end Doug Herman finally recovered it at the Houston two. Soon after, McCall took it over the goal line for the game winner with 5:52 left.

Brooks' team still had work to do to become a winner. But after pulling a bevy of bold moves, the coach was more likely to see it through.

Z IS FOR ZIMMERMAN

Offensive guard is not usually a position that goes noticed the way skill players are. But by his senior year in 1983, it was clear Gary Zimmerman was one of the best linemen in college football. He was a first-team All-American and elected by his peers as the Pacific-10 Conference's top offensive lineman. Zimmerman let the players around him—Mike Jorgensen, Lew Barnes, Ladaria Johnson—shine while he did the yeomanlike work of protecting them. Against California his senior year, though, he received a distinction very rare for an offensive lineman: Pac-10 player of the week.

As a Minnesota Viking, Zimmerman was voted the NFL's offensive lineman of the year in just his second season. He finished his career blocking for John Elway in the Denver Broncos' first Super Bowl win against Green Bay.

Since retiring, Zimmerman has become a fixture at Oregon home games, leading the team onto Autzen Stadium's Rich Brooks field atop his Harley Davidson motorcycle, cheerleaders lining his path and fight song blaring. Zimmerman's bike seems to symbolize the souped-up muscle of the program today.

TOO GOOD FOR FLAG FOOTBALL

In 1984, J.J. Birden was a star freshman football player—in intramural student flag football games. A former state champion sprinter at Lakeridge High School in suburban Portland, Birden and his former Lakeridge quarterback, Todd Boehm, starred for their freshman dorm's team against fraternities and other ragtag groups of students. "We had two plays: J.J. short, and J.J. deep," recalls Bob

Rickert, who today writes a Ducks blog for *The Oregonian.* "Boehm could chuck it 60 yards, and J.J. could run under it easily." One game pitted Birden and Boehm's flag team against a fraternity that included a redshirted Ducks player, Doug Judge. "J.J. beat Judge at least twice," Rickert adds, "and Judge all but dragged him to the practice field to make sure Rich Brooks talked to him."

Birden soon became a favorite target for both Chris Miller and Bill Musgrave. After being drafted by the NFL's Cleveland Browns in 1988, Birden wound up on the Kansas City Chiefs, catching passes from Joe Montana.

MILLER TIME

Between the Olympic Games in Los Angeles and the re-election of Ronald Reagan in 1984, the Oregon Ducks fielded their first winning side in four years at 6-5. But in the season opener at home, the team found itself losing in the first half by double digits to lowly Long Beach State. "We were getting thumped," coach Rich Brooks recalls. "We just weren't moving the ball."

Which is why Brooks relieved starter Mike Jorgensen with sophomore Chris Miller. In the next-to-last game the previous season, Miller had replaced an injured Jorgensen to lead Oregon over Stanford and quarterback John Elway 16-7. But Jorgensen had returned as the starter for 1984 until this fiasco in the works against the 49ers. Miller immediately began moving the offense downfield to ultimately retake the lead. Meanwhile, Brooks recalls, "We also started calling a lot of safety blitzes, because they had a hard time picking it up. We shut them down and they didn't score any more."

Even though he actually came from Eugene, Chris Miller had been a lucky and fairly rare blue-chip recruiting coup for Oregon. He was a three-sport star (football, basketball, and baseball) at Sheldon High School and a major prospect in all of them. But a knee injury his senior year had scared off some of the bigger programs interested in Miller's services.

After the Long Beach State win, Oregon continued rolling with victories over Colorado, Cal, and Pacific. The heart of the Pac-10 schedule took its toll as the Ducks suffered five losses in six games. However, a close 20-18 win against UCLA and a 31-6 steamrolling of OSU helped the team secure its third winning season under Brooks and the first since emerging from probation.

Meanwhile, Miller became the starter for good. He would ultimately throw for 6,841 yards and 42 touchdowns. "He was one of the most gifted athletes at that position I've ever coached," Brooks says. "He threw the ball accurately and he had enough arm strength that he could do it. But the key was just his athletic ability. If the protection broke down, he could escape trouble, break out of the pocket, and still get the ball down the field."

In 1987, Miller was picked 13th overall in the NFL draft's first round by the Atlanta Falcons and threw for over 19,000 yards with the Falcons, Rams, and Broncos before retiring in 1999.

BARNES AND CHERRY LOOM LARGE

Like past Oregon coaches such as Len Casanova, Rich Brooks often attracted top football talents who had been overlooked by more prestigious football programs because they were undersized. And in 1985, two of them were among the Ducks' biggest stars.

Standing 5-foot-7, Tony Cherry was the first Oregon running back in 12 years to surpass the 1,000-yard mark, and he did so in only nine full games. In the season opener at Washington State, Cherry was a workhorse, carrying 34 times for 143 yards in a narrow but dazzling 42-39 victory over a Cougar team led by future Super Bowl MVP Mark Rypien. "Oregon, With Cherry On Top, Ices WSU," ran the next morning's sports page headline in *The Oregonian*. Later that year, he carried the ball for 227 yards and three touchdowns against Stanford. He would finish the season with over 1,500 all-purpose yards.

Lew Barnes may have been the team's most popular player in 1985 thanks to his penchant for dazzling kick returns and pass receptions.

Often, the Autzen Stadium crowd seemed to be booing when Barnes made a big play, but they were actually calling his first name in tribute. Against San Diego State, he erupted for 185 yards, the second-most ever by a Duck receiver at the time. That year Barnes was a first-team All-American—one of only two Ducks to earn the distinction in a 17-year period between 1972 and 1988. Unfortunately, the trio of Miller, Barnes, and Cherry played during one of the only periods in Rich Brooks' tenure with porous defensive squads.

"They played their heart out," Brooks says of Cherry and Barnes. "These were some undersized guys, but more importantly they were exciting players, and they did a great job."

BOOKENDS

For the second straight year in 1986, Oregon narrowly missed a winning record, going 5-6 in Chris Miller's final campaign. Trouble came in the middle of the season, but memorable victories bookended the campaign. Against Colorado, Oregon amassed 368 yards but was trailing by a single point in the final moments when kicker Matt MacLeod booted the game winner for a 32-30 win. Oregon was 2-0 but then lost its next six, all to nationally ranked teams in an unlucky twist of scheduling fate.

The team rebounded to win its last three games, including a cathartic 49-28 victory against OSU at Parker Stadium in which Miller was almost flawless, completing 21 of 27 passes as the Ducks racked up 479 offensive yards on offense against Dave Kragthorpe's hapless Beavers. The losing season was a disappointment given Miller and the rest of the offensive squad's talents (not to mention the prowess of all-conference defensive back Anthony Newman). Miller would be taken 13th in the next spring's NFL draft, higher than any Oregon player since Bobby Moore. Waiting in the wings was a player who lacked Miller's physical talents, but more than made up for it in moxie—and wins.

THE FRESHMAN FROM GRAND JUNCTION

For four years at Autzen Stadium, from 1987-1990, fans developed an unlikely cheer. Each game, when public address announcer Don Essig named the radio affiliates of the Oregon Sports Network, the crowd roared for a small station in Grand Junction, Colorado. The station had added Duck games when a redshirt freshman from the town, a lanky redhead named Bill Musgrave, became the starting quarterback.

After Chris Miller graduated, most assumed his backup, Pete Nelson, would be starting. "He'd come in against Nebraska the year before when Chris Miller got hurt and threw the ball very well," coach Rich Brooks remembers. "And Pete was throwing it better than Musgrave in practice, at least in the drills. But every time we went into a scrimmage, Musgrave's team ended up scoring points. Every time he had the reins at quarterback, he got the team in the end zone. It was how the players responded to him in the huddle."

"I was not the most skilled passer on the team, that's for sure," agrees Musgrave. "There were guys who threw the ball a lot more naturally." But Musgrave had smarts and he was a leader. "As a quarterback, when you step into the huddle to call the play, you want to look in your teammates' eyes and know that they believe in you."

That belief would be rewarded, as the young man from Grand Junction would finish his career in Eugene as Oregon's all-time leader in passing and total offense, one of six quarterbacks in Pac-10 Conference history to throw for 8,000 yards and 60 or more touchdowns. More importantly, Bill Musgrave would help guide a resurgence that would see the Ducks football program earn its first bowl berth in more than a quarter-century.

First, though, as fall camp came to a close in 1987, Brooks had to make a leap of faith: handing over the offensive reins to a freshman. "It wasn't unanimous among the coaches, but I made the decision that Musgrave was going to start for us because I felt that he had that

Quarterback Bill Musgrave.
Image courtesy of Special Collections and University Archives, University of Oregon libraries

intangible quality," the coach remembers. "He was just one of those guys who I like to call a winner."

TENDERFOOT TAMES BUFFALOES

The Ducks were a two-touchdown underdog in Boulder to begin the 1987 season against Colorado, the last of four straight years pitting Oregon against the Buffaloes (each decided by less than a touchdown). Redshirt freshman quarterback Bill Musgrave did just enough to help turn a heroic defensive effort into a 10-7 win.

Despite the challenge of beginning his college career on the road against a Big 8 Conference power, 19-year-old Musgrave wasn't daunted. "I think it was natural for me to be ready to hit the ground running with that first game," he remembers. "Really, the toughest year of my athletic life was the year that I redshirted, because I wasn't involved in the games. So I was excited to get back to doing what I truly enjoyed: competing."

On the other side of the ball, defensive coordinator Denny Schuler installed a new, more aggressive 3-4 scheme. Led by such standouts as cornerback Anthony Newman and linemen Matt Brock and Rollin Putzier, the defense held Colorado to a single touchdown the entire game.

Musgrave got off to a quick start. "He takes our opening drive as a first-time starter in a major college game and drives us 80 yards for a touchdown," Brooks recalls. The recipient was another underclassman with many great moments ahead: sophomore receiver Terry Obee.

But it was a fellow redshirt freshman of Musgrave's, offensive guard Andy Sunia, who caused the head coach to both scowl and smile. With Oregon facing third and goal from the Colorado two-yard line, Sunia jumped offsides. On the ensuing play from the seven, Musgrave found Obee for the sole Duck touchdown of the game.

"We come off the field and everybody's celebrating, but Andy Sunia's on the bench bawling like a baby," Brooks laughs, remembering. "I said, 'What's the matter?' He said, 'Coach, I let you down. I came offsides.' And I said, 'That's okay, we overcame it!'"

BACK-TO-BACK DUELS

By 1987, Oregon's rivalry against Washington was perhaps at its most lopsided, with the Huskies having won six straight and 12 of 13. With coach Don James' team boasting a Heisman Trophy candidate in quarterback Chris Chandler, it was no surprise to see a large contingent of Husky fans making the trip south on Interstate 5 to Autzen Stadium for the game.

But this was a new era for Oregon, which had a talented quarterback of its own in redshirt freshman Bill Musgrave. And the team had come up with a tight victory the week before. "We had to put together a 90-yard two-minute drive into the wind to beat San Diego State, which gave us even more confidence going into the Washington game," Bill Musgrave recalls. "There's a lot to be said for a young team trying to find its identity, and that's what we were at that time."

Washington took an early 7-0 lead in the first quarter, but it didn't take Oregon long to respond. On the Ducks' first play from scrimmage after the Husky touchdown, Musgrave hit Terry Obee with a short pass, and Obee raced untouched for an 82-yard score. Later in the half, Oregon took a lead it would not relinquish, holding on 29-22 to avenge the string of losses.

The next week, USC came to Eugene with another Heisman candidate and future NFL quarterback, Rodney Pete. Going into the game the Ducks were 3-1, their only loss a respectable 24-14 showing on the road versus mighty Ohio State. Musgrave guided Oregon to an astonishing 21-0 lead against Southern Cal. Like Washington the week before, the Trojans rallied, but not before Rich Brooks' team had secured a 34-27 win.

Unfortunately, the seemingly red-hot Ducks then went on to lose four straight games, including a lopsided 41-10 affair against UCLA. A winning season in jeopardy at 4-5 with two games to go, Oregon earned a hard-fought 31-17 victory in the Palouse against Washington State and then produced a 44-0 blowout in the Civil War. The team had salvaged a winning season at 6-5 but its bowl eligibility was not answered with an invitation, continuing a postseason drought dating to the 1963 Sun Bowl. Still, Oregon finally had the makings of a perennially winning program.

POOLING THEIR RESOURCE

When Bill Musgrave took over the starting quarterback job as a freshman, it didn't stop the first-year player from getting hazed by his upperclassmen teammates. On Sunday afternoons, many players went to Lane Pool and used its hot tub to soothe the soreness of full-contact football the day before. As quarterback, Musgrave was invited, but perhaps with devious motives. "They would throw me in the pool with my clothes on," Musgrave recalls. During away games, the young signal caller also found himself occasionally locked in hotel elevators. "Those guys like big Rollin Putzier, Devin Fitzpatrick, Tom Talbott, and Mike Blakey, I don't think they knew quite what to do with a 185-pound freshman quarterback on the other side," he adds. "But it was worth it, because they were quite a group on defense."

GANGLAND STOMPING

Although Oregon wasn't invited to a bowl game at the end of the 1987 season, a victory over Oregon State made the Ducks bowl eligible at 6-5. And that sixth win came in emphatic fashion.

"The University of Oregon Ducks pounded Oregon State 44-0 today in what looked like a merciless, gangland stomping before a crowd of 43,157 at Autzen Stadium," reported Ken Goe of *The Oregonian*. It had been the most lopsided Civil War contest since 1895.

Derek Loville scored Oregon's first two touchdowns, augmented by two Kirk Dennis field goals and fullback Latin Berry's eight-yard touchdown run to put the Ducks ahead 27-0 at halftime. In the third quarter, Musgrave threw a four-yard touchdown pass to tight end Joe Meerten, Dennis added another field goal, and James Harper scampered into the end zone from 13 yards out.

Following Harper's score, Oregon State ran the ensuing kickoff in for a touchdown, but the play was called back on a clipping penalty. It was that kind of day for the Beavers, who saw both quarterbacks Erik Wilhelm and Kent Riddle knocked out of the game.

Running back Derek Loville.
Image courtesy of Special Collections and University Archives, University of Oregon libraries

Oregon, meanwhile, finished year one of the Musgrave era with a very large exclamation point.

REVERSAL OF FORTUNE

In 1988, Oregon took a 5-1 record into its game with Washington after lopsided wins against Long Beach State, Washington State, and Idaho State. The Ducks were also coming off a win the year before against their rivals from Seattle, and a scheduling anomaly put the game at Autzen for a second straight season.

Still, beating UW was a tall order. "The Huskies at that time were a nationally ranked team all the time," Rich Brooks recalls. "Don James had them really going."

Late in the fourth quarter, Washington led 14-10 and could have been ahead by more had Oregon cornerback Ron Gould not intercepted a Husky pass in the end zone. In the game's final moments, Bill Musgrave guided the team into striking distance. The UW defense tightened, and Oregon faced fourth down and one yard to go inside the Husky five. Send star running back Derek Loville up the middle? Not with Washington's best defensive player, monstrous lineman Dennis Brown, waiting at the line of scrimmage.

Instead, offensive coordinator Bob Toledo proposed a bold but risky move. "Bob looked at me and said, 'What do you think about calling the reverse?'" Brooks remembers. "And I said, 'Let's go for it.'"

"I took the play back into the huddle and the players were excited," Musgrave remembers. "Everyone's hair stood up on the back of their necks. We were ready to make it work."

Musgrave faked a handoff up the middle, where Brown was in the process of breaking through the line. Receiver Terry Obee looped behind the quarterback, took the ball, and sprinted for the corner of the goal line. The Huskies' Brown "was the only one who really had a chance," Brooks says. "Everybody else was sucked into the middle, thinking we were going to run. Obee ran around with Dennis Brown chasing him into the end zone." And the bulging lineman was not going to catch the speedy receiver.

Oregon won 17-14 and was brimming with confidence. But in a heartbreaking twist of fate, this would be the Ducks' last win of the season.

BROKEN COLLARBONE, BROKEN SEASON

After the Washington win and a No. 20 spot in the Associated Press poll, Oregon seemed to be on its way to something special. The team had all-conference players at many skill positions and its future all-time passing leader just coming into his own as a sophomore. "We had a fantastic defense, and on offense we had matured from the year before," Bill Musgrave says. "I don't think it'd be any stretch to say that was the best team in my four years at Oregon."

Oregon was favored against the Sun Devils, but was losing in the fourth quarter when Musgrave drove the team inside the 10-yard line. Then tragedy struck. Musgrave kept the ball on an option play and suffered a broken collarbone. He was done for the season. Oregon not only lost that Saturday, but would also finish the year with five losses in Musgrave's absence. That included the Ducks' first Civil War loss since 1974 to an Oregon State team occupying the Pac-10 Conference cellar with coach Jerry Pettibone's antiquated wishbone offense.

"We were playing well against ASU that day," Musgrave remembers. "It was going to be a dogfight because they were keeping pace with us. But we were on our way to one heck of a season, maybe the kind of season that Oregon hadn't seen for a while and then ultimately saw in the mid-'90s."

The next week, Oregon faced UCLA in a nationally televised game that had been marketed as a duel between two of the conference's hottest quarterbacks: Musgrave and the Bruins' Troy Aikman. Instead, Pete Nelson lined up under center. Led by a stout defense, the Ducks hung tough with UCLA and its future NFL Hall of Fame quarterback, but ultimately lost a hard-fought contest 16-6.

The Jekyll-and-Hyde nature of the 1988 season typifies the promise and peril Oregon teams showed during this era as the Ducks slowly clawed their way back to a winning program after two decades of disappointment. "We didn't have a lot of the depth that other teams have," Brooks says of the ill-fated '88 squad. "But it was a heck of a football team."

5

BACK IN BOWLS
1989-1995

OVERDUE BILL

THE LAST TIME Bill Musgrave had played quarterback for the Ducks in 1988, the team was 6-1. With the junior finally healthy to begin the 1989 season, the squad was eager to pick up where it left off.

First Oregon knocked off Cal 35-19 in its season opener at Autzen, following up with an eye-opening road win against Hayden Fry's Iowa Hawkeyes, 44-6. "That was a big road trip for us and a big win," Musgrave remembers. "We had an experienced group going into the game. The offensive line was rolling, and we had really the best set of running backs you could ask for in Derek [Loville] and Latin [Berry]. Joe Merton had emerged as quite a threat at tight end. It was a heck of a team we had going."

But the Iowa win was also costly, as the Ducks lost two players, Berry and center Scot Boatright, to season-ending injuries. "It was tough to get on that plane and come home knowing those guys wouldn't be with us for the rest of the year," Musgrave continues. "At that time, depth was a concern and the hangover from those injuries stayed with us for a week or two. We were up on Stanford, and we lost our focus."

Indeed, Oregon lost to the Cardinal after being up 17 points. And it wasn't even the team's biggest blown lead of the year. Against

Brigham Young and record-breaking quarterback Ty Detmer in Provo, Oregon would see a 19-point lead disintegrate in a marathon 45-41 loss. Funnily enough, however, the heartbreaking defeat seemed to be just the tonic Oregon needed. At 5-4 after the BYU loss, it was make or break time for the season. Becoming the starter as a freshman two seasons before, Musgrave had been a kind of golden boy. Injuries had curtailed his first two years, but the junior quarterback now had the opportunity to fulfill his promise.

LOVILLE AT FIRST SIGHT

The success Chris Miller and Bill Musgrave enjoyed at quarterback from 1986-1989 was made possible in large part because of an upgraded running attack led by Derek Loville. Despite sharing carries with another talented back of the same class, Latin Berry, Loville rewrote the Oregon record books, becoming the Ducks' all-time leader in yards, scoring, touchdowns, and all-purpose yardage. He was also the first player in team history to lead the Ducks in rushing four straight years. In 1988, Loville became Oregon's first back in three seasons to surpass 1,000 yards. Against Idaho State that year, he gained 215 yards on just 23 carries for a better than nine-yard average. In a tough road game at Arizona State the next season, Loville gained another 203 yards, helping to propel the team to four wins in its last five and an Independence Bowl berth.

Viewed by NFL scouts as undersized, Loville went undrafted, but proved his doubters wrong with a 10-year career with the San Francisco 49ers and Denver Broncos, winning Super Bowl rings in both stops.

MAKING THE BOWL HAPPEN

When the Ducks received interest from the Poulan Weed Eater Independence Bowl following its 7-4 regular season in 1989, the school had a selling job to do. Bowl games are business as much as sport, and with Oregon not having played a bowl game since 1963, organizers of the Shreveport, Louisiana, contest sought assurances from the Ducks athletic department that an acceptable number of fans would cross the country for it. To secure the invitation, athletic director Bill Byrne committed the university to purchasing 14,000 tickets.

Oregon fans, ecstatic over their team's first postseason appearance in a generation, made a strong showing in Shreveport despite frigid conditions. It wasn't Pasadena, but the Duck faithful were far from pretentious. This was cause for celebration. The athletic department still took a loss from the endeavor, albeit without regret.

"The Independence Bowl was a huge, huge step forward for Oregon," Brooks says. "That game as much as anything turned Oregon's football fortunes. We showed our fans cared and they followed the team."

"I think it proved sometimes you have to spend money to make money," Musgrave adds. "Bill Byrne really kind of speculated on the football program and almost underwrote the trip. Everything blossoms from that point, but he got our foot in the door there. It really kind of launched the entire program."

INDEPENDENCE NIGHT

Oregon's 27-24 victory over Tulsa in the Independence Bowl December 16, 1989, may not have captured the nation's imagination. It was a lower-tier bowl in Shreveport, Louisiana, on a night with temperatures below freezing. But Oregon's Independence Bowl win was a cathartic validation that, after years of frustration, the program had been turned around.

It proved the culminating moment in the career of one of the team's all-time greatest players, Bill Musgrave, and it brought redemption to a head coach who had been knocking on the postseason door for 12 years. But that was nothing: Ducks fans themselves had been waiting all the way back to 1963.

"We were so excited to be going to a bowl game," says Musgrave. "And we didn't care whether one bowl was better than another. It was the ultimate for us to go to Shreveport. I know that people in the crowd still talk to this day about how cold that was. But I don't think any of us players were even aware of it."

Tensions were running high at an Independence Bowl function a few nights before the game. "They introduced both sides' starters," Brooks recalls. "When Joe Farwell was introduced, the Tulsa players started making fun of him because he was relatively small and he looked like a college professor or something. That kind of pissed our team off. Farwell was one of the best linebackers around."

Perhaps because of the emotion, this transformative night for the Oregon football program didn't start out well. Despite the Ducks leading in most statistical categories, Tulsa led on the scoreboard for the first three quarters. It was 24-17 heading into the fourth, Tulsa's advantage aided by two interceptions and a blocked punt returned for a touchdown. "They had a lot of guys who ended up in the NFL," Brooks adds. "They were very physical."

But key defensive plays such as Chris Oldham's two interceptions kept Oregon in the game. And behind Musgrave, the offense played its best when the game was on the line, scoring 17 points in the last 18 minutes. First the quarterback hit Joe Reitzug from nine yards out with 2:05 left in the third quarter after completing five of six passes on the key 54-yard drive. Then Musgrave scored from one yard out to tie the score with 12:38 left in the game, hoisting his arms into the air in a rare display of emotion. And why not? It was both the tying score and the first rushing touchdown of Musgrave's entire Oregon career.

After the Duck defense stopped multiple Tulsa drives, kicker Gregg McCallum won the game with a 20-yard field goal at 3:07. With 22 seconds remaining, Matt LaBounty's 26-yard sack of Golden Hurricanes quarterback Matt Adams put an exclamation point on the game—an ideal stat considering it had been 26 years since the last Oregon bowl victory.

Defensive back Chris Oldham celebrates against Washington.
Image courtesy of Special Collections and University Archives, University of Oregon libraries

EXTRA EFFORT AND INCHES SHORT

Oregon's 8-3 regular-season record in 1990 could have been 9-2 if not for the slimmest of margins on one particular play. With the Ducks trailing 22-17 in the final seconds against Arizona, Bill Musgrave raced for the goal line but was stopped just inches short. The difference in the game may have been an injury Oregon's quarterback suffered the night before, after practice.

"Everyone else had gone into the locker room," he recalls. "But I was working on some footwork after practice with our defensive end, Jeff Cummins. He'd simulate rushing the passer so I could work on moving in and out of the pocket. But I twisted my ankle. I was so frustrated and upset with myself. The whole night I was up with our trainer, Dean Adams, trying to ice my ankle and get it right. But it wasn't right for the game. At the end I was trying to run for the corner, and their All-America cornerback, Daryl Lewis, put a hit on me. It was a good hit, but if I was running on two good ankles I could have made that. It's been a big regret all these years."

In Musgrave's defense, Oregon never would have reached a second straight bowl game that year without his efforts—including staying after practice to work on footwork drills. It didn't work out in Arizona, but the way No. 14 was playing his senior year, few Ducks supporters could complain.

A WIN AGAINST TY

Brigham Young came to Autzen Stadium on September 29, 1990, with a No. 4 ranking and that year's Heisman Trophy winner-to-be, Ty Detmer. Coach Lavelle Edwards' Cougars left licking their paws.

Oregon was eager to avenge its loss to BYU in a 45-41 shootout the year before. "It was an incredible scene at Autzen, bright sunshine and not a cloud in the sky," Musgrave remembers. "We got there early, like we always would for the game. You could smell the paper and the pulp from Weyerhaeuser. I just remember so many senses from that day."

In the previous meeting, Musgrave and Detmer had broken the NCAA record for combined passing yards. In the sequel, however, defense would have a bigger impact. Led by players like Matt LaBounty, Andy Conner, and Eric Castle, Oregon was ferocious against Detmer, its constant pressure forcing the quarterback into five interceptions. Marcus Woods also sacked Detmer for a safety. The BYU quarterback still managed to throw for a robust 442 yards, but didn't yield enough points as Oregon regularly tightened inside the red zone. Musgrave, meanwhile, threw less often than Detmer while Sean Burwell amassed 104 yards on the ground, but Oregon's quarterback was the more accurate passer, hitting 23 for 27. In the end, Musgrave outplayed his more heralded counterpart and the Ducks won easily, 32-16. "Ty's become a good friend in the years since," Musgrave says, "and we always wind up recounting those two games."

HIS LAST PASS A TOUCHDOWN

Every Oregon senior likes his last game at Autzen Stadium to be a memorable one. And for quarterback Bill Musgrave, his finalé in Eugene came with a storybook ending.

The opponent was UCLA, which, behind quarterback Tommy Maddox, led for the first three and a half quarters, including 24-13 with 9:13 remaining in the game. "Tommy was throwing balls all over the yard that night," Musgrave recalls. But after struggling all day, Oregon's offense was just coming alive.

First, the Ducks drove 72 yards to close within three points, capped by fullback Juan Shedrick's touchdown and little-used Ngalu Kelemeni's two-point conversion. After the defense forced the Bruins to punt, Oregon began its next possession at the UCLA 45 thanks to Brian Brown's long punt return. Two plays later, tailback Sean Burwell took a Musgrave screen pass 28 yards to the Bruin 17—after setting a key block to buy his quarterback enough time to throw.

A version of the same play, only with a twist, accounted for the winning score. This time, offensive coordinator Mike Bellotti's screen had the tight end going out for a pass instead of blocking—a "wheel route." Not only was it risky giving Musgrave less protection, but starting tight end Jeff Thomason was also out of the game with a broken ankle. His backup, sophomore Vince Ferry, hadn't even earned a letter yet. He was also playing with a cast on his arm.

But Ferry certainly earned an 'O' for his jacket after catching in the end zone the last pass thrown at Autzen Stadium by Oregon's all-time leading passer—and a game winner at that.

"Vince went down into the corner by the cheerleaders and caught a ball right in the cover-two honey hole," Musgrave says, describing the coverage. "He just made a fantastic catch. And I wasn't the best pure thrower, but that ball came out of my hand pretty clean. It kind of frozen-roped there in the air. It looked like a Chris Miller pass to me: the ball didn't have a lot of arc to it, but it was clean and it got from A to B in a hurry. I think that I finally cut one loose."

After the game, the sellout crowd of 45,901 did some cutting loose of its own—with the Autzen goalpost.

FREEDOM ISN'T FREE

Oregon's performance in the 1990 Freedom Bowl against Colorado State included some incredible individual moments and performances, but ultimately amounted to a bitter loss.

Oregon was excited for a second straight bowl—and a slightly more prestigious one than last year's Independence Bowl, at that—within driving distance for many of the 17,500 Duck fans who helped fill Anaheim Stadium. "The Oregon contingent was really rocking up there," Musgrave remembers. "We could see those upper decks kind of swaying with everybody cheering."

Musgrave set numerous Freedom Bowl records, going 29 of 47 passing with 392 yards, which included what was almost the game-winning score. After trailing 32-25 with under five minutes remaining, Oregon marched 79 yards for a touchdown on the strength of two Joe Reitzug catches for 31 and 21 yards and a culminating Sean Burwell one-yard score with just 61 seconds left. Coach Rich Brooks decided Oregon would go for the win with a two-point conversion attempt instead of kicking the extra point for the tie.

Musgrave actually completed the conversion attempt to senior flanker Michael McClellan in the end zone, but McClellan was immediately pushed out by Colorado State defenders. The officials ruled that the ball had not crossed the plane of the end zone, and thus the conversion was no good. After a failed onsides kick, Earl Bruce's team ran out the clock. To this day, some Duck fans refuse to accept the 32-31 score.

"I threw it a little bit too far outside of Michael McClellan," the former quarterback says. "That's a tough way to end an exciting game that had gone back and forth. Joe Reitzug had some gutsy catches in there and we racked up a bunch of yards. We went up and down the field."

As exasperating as the two-point conversion play may have been, it was only one in a long line of near misses and mistakes that even today seem to eat away at those Oregon personnel involved. "Sean Burwell dropped the ball twice without ever being hit," Brooks offers. "One of them, he's got a hole almost as wide as the freeway going off of right tackle. He's into the secondary and the only guy between him and the end zone is the safety. He kind of does a little shake move and the ball comes out of his hand, and they recover it."

All told, the Ducks suffered three fumbles and a muffed punt. A roughing the passer penalty was also as costly as a turnover in changing a forced punting situation to a first down for the Rams. The 32 surrendered points belied a valiant effort by Oregon's defense, led by sophomore inside linebacker Joe Farwell's game-high 15 tackles. And then there was Musgrave, whose statistics were spectacular in the losing effort. Oregon led Colorado State in both first downs and total yards, despite having only seven yards rushing. It came down to No. 14's passing.

"He laid it on the field and gave everything he had, and he made a lot of really good plays," Brooks says. "We just made too many errors to win the game. We basically gave that game away."

Still, nobody could take anything away from the group of players who had secured for Oregon a second straight bowl appearance after a generation of coming up short. It was also the end of an era as the team said goodbye to its all-time leading passer, who had started for four straight years and turned in his jersey to a program transformed. By no means had Bill Musgrave done it alone. There were skill players around him, like Derek Loville, Tony Hargain (one of Oregon's only top-rated recruits), and Terry Obee, as well as defensive players, including Chris Oldham and Matt LaBounty. Still, there's no question these were the Bill Musgrave years.

Although his career in the NFL consisted almost solely of backup status, Musgrave later put his offensive smarts to work as a longtime quarterbacks coach and offensive coordinator for a number of pro franchises. He credits his second career to long hours spent with offensive coordinator Bob Toledo (later UCLA's head coach) in the coach's MacArthur Court office.

"I often catch myself wishing that I knew then what I know now," he says. "If I knew certain aspects about defense or pass patterns like I've learned in the last 10 or 15 years, if I knew that when I was playing, I really could have used that knowledge, Xs and Os-wise. But you also think back to that time when you're 19, 20, 21 years old and how you feel invincible. I would never trade those feelings or those instincts for the world. That was, of course, for a lot of us, the best time of our lives, going to school there in Eugene and playing Pac-10 football."

DIFFICULT TRANSITION

Optimism was high among Duck fans who packed Autzen Stadium for the 1991 season. Bill Musgrave was gone, but freshman quarterback Danny O'Neil seemed to follow in his footsteps with an improbably hot start. Oregon bested Washington State 40-14 at home and Texas Tech 28-13 on the road behind four O'Neil touchdown passes.

O'Neil had been recruited out of Newport Beach, California, by Brooks' assistant Nick Aliotti. "He was very good at highlighting the way Oregon was a program up-and-coming," O'Neil remembers. "I remember in particular he showed me the offensive stat sheets from the years before under Bill Musgrave. It was clear Oregon did well offensively." But as much as football prowess, the quarterback from Southern California was drawn to the area's natural beauty. "I liked the open country and the mountains better than I liked skyscrapers. You had both snow skiing and the ocean that were really close. I ended up picking Oregon over places like Alabama and USC because of that."

After O'Neil's promising start, though, the team's fortunes tumbled. Oregon would record just one victory in its last nine games. And in that lone victory, 29-6 against lowly New Mexico State, O'Neil was lost for the season to a dislocated thumb. A 3-2 record would become 3-8 as a string of quarterbacks failed to produce: Brett Saisbury, Kyle Crowston, Bob Brothers (son of former Beaver quarterback Paul Brothers), and even Bill Musgrave's younger brother, Doug. In the season finale, Oregon lost at home to an Oregon State team with a record of 0-10 going into the game. It was the Beavers' first win against Oregon since 1971.

"It was a difficult time for me, and the program went through a lot of criticism," O'Neil adds. "It ended on a very sour note."

But the young quarterback was just getting started. A mix of failure and success still lay ahead, and before his career was over, O'Neil would lead Oregon to a Promised Land that legendary Duck quarterbacks like Musgrave, Dan Fouts, and Bob Berry never reached.

MIDDLE OF THE PAC

Amidst Bill Clinton's successful White House campaign against President George H.W. Bush, 1992 saw Rich Brooks' team return to the Independence Bowl for the second time in four years. But this time, the euphoria was replaced by unfulfilled hopes. "I think a good synopsis of those years is that Oregon seemed to always beat the teams we were supposed to beat, but rarely beat the teams we weren't supposed to beat," recalls Danny O'Neil of his sophomore and junior seasons.

The team got off to a terrible start that year, losing to both Hawaii and Stanford. But as they would do two years later en route to the Rose Bowl, Rich Brooks' young squad bounced back. A three-game winning streak began with a narrow 16-13 decision against Texas Tech, then gained steam with a 59-6 pounding of UNLV and a solid 30-20 win against Arizona State. From here, however, the Ducks played up and down with a 3-3 finish that included a rainy 7-0 Civil War victory on the puddle-strewn Astroturf of Parker Stadium. At 6-5, Oregon secured an invitation to the Independence Bowl, site of the team's joyous comeback win three years earlier. This time, though, Oregon blew a 19-point third-quarter lead to lose 39-35.

For nearly three quarters in Shreveport against Wake Forest, Oregon played some of its best football of the season. In the first period, Sean Burwell scampered for a 40-yard touchdown and cornerback Herman O'Berry returned a fumble 24 yards for another score. O'Neil's touchdown pass to Vince Ferry and a Tommy Thompson field goal gave Oregon a 22-10 halftime lead. O'Berry's counterpart in the defensive backfield, future All-American Alex Molden, added an eight-yard interception and touchdown just over five minutes into the second half. But the 29-10 lead didn't last as Oregon's defense suddenly wilted amidst four straight Wake Forest touchdowns. In only about 15 minutes of game time, the Ducks' 19-point lead had incredibly become a 10-point deficit. O'Neil's touchdown pass to Ronnie Harris with a minute left was as far as Oregon could come back for a stunning 39-35 loss.

"I felt like I'd played better my sophomore year and our team had more success, but it was still incredibly disappointing because of difficult losses," O'Neil says. "It all comes down to—for me as a young quarterback or anybody—you don't have a lot of leeway. I needed to play better if our team was going to have more success."

ONE STEP BACK

Things started out well in 1993. In its opener at Colorado State, Oregon avenged a bitter Freedom Bowl loss from three years before. A surprisingly narrow 35-30 home win over Montana was followed by a more impressive non-conference road win, this time against Illinois of the Big Ten. Rich Brooks and company felt reason to be optimistic heading to Berkeley's Strawberry Canyon for an October 2 matchup with Cal. And sure enough, after the O'Neil-led offense built a 31-0 first-half lead, a 4-0 start seemed a foregone conclusion. But just as they'd done against Wake Forest 10 months before, the Duck defense imploded.

Led by quarterback Dave Barr, Cal's ferocious second-half comeback was the biggest in Pac-10 Conference history and one point shy of an NCAA record. Final score: 42-41. Instead of being undefeated, a humiliated Oregon team was on its way to losing five of seven. And the mental strain seemed to affect the team's entire season. Danny O'Neil actually became only the fourth Pac-10 quarterback to throw for more than 3,000 yards that year, but in large part because his team was so often behind. Oregon never quite recovered psychologically from the Cal loss.

As has so often happened in the history of the Oregon program, though, great success began amidst the ashes of disappointment. After the promise of the Musgrave years, the program hoped to turn the corner and join the nation's elite. It hadn't happened quite that way, at least not at first. But by this point, athletic director Bill Byrne had spearheaded a series of investments in Oregon's facilities to aid recruiting, such as the Len Casanova Center that housed new training and locker facilities for the team in the latest architectural arms race in college football. It was a far cry from the days when Brooks' staff used to hold meetings in the Autzen Stadium tunnel, diagramming plays on the wall like ancient cave paintings.

What's more, the talented young players who had made the last two years frustratingly uneven were ready to come of age. Oregon's class of 1994 had little to show for the first three years of its college football career, but would finish in historic fashion.

A TURNAROUND FOR THE AGES

If the Oregon Ducks' historic Rose Bowl season in 1994 turned out to be a fairy tale, then its plot complication came early in the story. Rich Brooks' team demolished Division 1-AA Portland State 58-16 in its opener, but the next two weeks both produced losses for Oregon, first against Hawaii and then Utah. The team also lost Corey Murphy to a career-ending spinal cord injury against the Rainbow Warriors. Oregon was 1-2 to begin the new year and, with the team coming off a disappointing 3-8 season, Brooks' job was called into question. "That's when the wolves started howling for my scalp," the coach recalls.

What no one could have predicted was the incredible turnaround about to take place. "Those losses brought the character of that team more to the forefront," quarterback Danny O'Neil says. "You either turn and run or come together and fight. The players and coaches still believed we could be a special group. We had some player-led meetings, which I don't remember happening before in my four years there. I remember people saying, 'Nobody believes in us, but we believe we can win football games. Let's just all go do our jobs and get it done.'"

On paper, things seemed even tougher the next week when a Big Ten Conference opponent, Hayden Fry's Iowa Hawkeyes, would arrive in town. But this was the 1994 Ducks' coming-out party. To nearly everyone's surprise except the Oregon players, Brooks' team won 40-

Defensive back Kenny Wheaton's game-saving interception against Washington in 1994 propelled Oregon into the Rose Bowl race. *Image provided by John Giustina*

18. "Everybody was ready to start throwing dirt on our grave, and our players just wouldn't accept that," Brooks says.

If the Iowa win was a surprise, the next week's 23-7 victory against USC was an outright shocker. The Ducks hadn't won at Los Angeles Memorial Coliseum since 1971, and they would have to face the Trojans without quarterback Danny O'Neil, who developed an unexpected finger infection. Tailback Ricky Whittle and cornerback Herman O'Berry were also missing. But each player's replacement was a star that day. Backup quarterback Tony Graziani (who would start the following season) threw for 287 yards, with tight end Josh Wilcox a key target. Dino Philyaw rushed for 123 yards, including a dramatic 49-yard touchdown. And then there was freshman cornerback Kenny Wheaton, who foreshadowed the heroics of his famous interception versus Washington two games later with an incredible pick against the Trojans. USC receiver Mark Grace appeared to have made the reception, but Wheaton simply tore the ball from his grasp in stride. "Kenny Wheaton stole that football," Brooks says. "It looked like the receiver had it and was running, and all of a sudden Wheaton's running the other way."

"That was one of my best plays in my career," Wheaton says. "Plus it was my first time ever playing a Pac-10 game. We went down there and no one gave us a chance—*no one*. We probably had guys on the team whose parents didn't believe we'd win. And it came down to three of us who weren't even supposed to play. It gave each of us a jump-start in our careers."

Not only that, but Oregon had lifted itself off the canvas and had come back fighting. After starting 1-2, Rich Brooks' team would go 8-1 to finish the 1994 regular season. But first, some of the team's all-time most historic games were still to be played.

MARCH TO THE ROSE BOWL

As dramatic as the 1994 Washington game and Kenny Wheaton's interception (see Prologue) would be considered regardless of the circumstances, the win also propelled Oregon into the driver's seat for the Rose Bowl race. Win out and they'd earn a trip to Pasadena. But there wasn't much time to daydream. After Washington, the Ducks faced another Rose Bowl favorite in Arizona, which had drubbed Miami in the Fiesta Bowl the year before on the strength of its renowned "Desert Swarm" defense led by Tedy Bruschi.

Oregon, however, now had a nickname-worthy defense of its own: Gang Green. Led by players like Chad Cota, Reggie Jordan, Jeremy Asher, and Alex Molden, the defense relied on the ability of its cornerbacks to play single coverage against opposing receivers, thus enabling relentless line pressure and blitzing. Gang Green helped keep the Arizona game a low-scoring affair, but the Wildcats still led 6-3 at halftime. Yet after having successfully come from behind in dramatic fashion the week before, the Ducks remained confident.

"At halftime I said to the defense, 'We'll score against these guys—I can guarantee you. But you can't give up many more points,'" O'Neil remembers. "And that's what happened."

Arizona had built a 9-3 lead in the fourth quarter, but O'Neil hit tight end Josh Wilcox in the end zone for a 10-9 Ducks lead. Gang Green held on for the victory. "The fact that we were able to shut them down as well as we did defensively was really huge," Brooks says.

The remaining games suddenly took on new meaning. "Now it wasn't just a normal football game that you wanted to win," O'Neil says. "The Rose Bowl was on the line. We're left with three teams that we should beat, but that we know can also beat us if we're not careful."

Oregon decided the next two games early, throttling Arizona State 34-10 at home and Stanford 55-21 in Palo Alto, the latter of which sounded practically like Eugene, thanks to a growing Ducks bandwagon that made the 10-hour drive to the Bay Area. By this time, former Oregon greats like Ahmad Rashad even began to hang out on the sidelines. The two blowouts gave the Ducks time to recharge batteries before the wrenching drama everyone saw coming: a Civil War in Corvallis.

Oregon State was 4-6 going into the game, but the annual Ducks-Beavers contest is almost always close. And while a winning season was already impossible, OSU certainly had something to play for. "They could have made their whole season by stopping us from winning our first outright championship in school history," Brooks says.

"To think we may lose to Oregon State and not go to the Rose Bowl was such a scary and frightening feeling," O'Neil agrees. "But you have to go back to the character of that team. We believed we were a good football team even before we actually were a good football team. We were ready and prepared to deal with that pressure."

"LOOKING FOR SOMEONE TO HUG"

November 19, 1994, was a day Oregon fans had awaited for a generation. The team had rebounded from its losing ways of the 1970s and early '80s with bowl games after the 1989, '90, and '92 seasons. Now the stakes were significantly higher. If able to beat their century-long archrival, the Ducks and their fans would be on their way to Oregon's first Rose Bowl in 37 years.

Jerry Pettibone's Beavers were adept at controlling the ball, and a solid defense helped keep games close. For much of the 1994 Civil War against the Ducks, however, Pettibone's team did more than stay close—they led.

Trailing Oregon State 13-10, the Ducks took the ball at their own 30-yard line with 4:42 left in the game. O'Neil had already answered his critics, leading Oregon to comeback wins against Washington and Arizona. Could he and the team do it again?

"We got the ball back and pretty much everybody figured this would be our last chance," O'Neil remembers. "If we don't score here, there's a good chance we wouldn't get the ball again. It all came down to that one drive. We either get it done or we don't."

Luckily for the Ducks, go-to receiver Cristin McLemore was back in the game. McLemore had become Oregon's all-time leading receiver against Stanford the week before. In the third quarter versus the

Beavers, though, his left hand had been crushed against teammate Ricky Whittle's helmet. After McLemore was taken by golf cart to the Oregon State infirmary for X-rays, several suspicious minutes went by in which school officials couldn't seem to find an X-ray technician.

On that final possession, though, McLemore was instrumental. He caught a 31-yard pass to begin the drive, cradling the ball against his chest with his good hand. Two plays later, O'Neil found McLemore again, this time on the left sideline for 21 yards. For a moment, the tension was eased on a hilarious offsides call in which tight end Josh Wilcox lost his balance and fell backwards onto his behind.

Then came one of the biggest plays in Oregon football history. At the Beaver 21-yard line with 3:43 left, O'Neil threw a screen pass to running back Dino Philyaw, who sprinted virtually untouched into the Beaver end zone. Finally, the Ducks had retaken the lead against Oregon State in a Civil War with the Rose Bowl on the line. But with plenty of time left even for the overwhelmingly run-oriented Beaver offense to take advantage, the game wasn't over. Oregon State drove from its own 15 to Oregon's 21, and in the final seconds, quarterback Don Shanklin lofted a wobbly pass toward the Oregon goal line. But the ball fell harmlessly incomplete, and the jubilant Ducks took over on downs to run out the clock.

As the final gun sounded, Oregon players hoisted coach Rich Brooks onto their shoulders, while others clutched long-stemmed red roses in celebration. Brooks would win numerous national Coach of the Year honors that season, which he quickly shrugged off. "One week you've got rope burns on your neck," he told *Sports Illustrated*, recalling how fans had called for his firing earlier that year, "and the next you're somebody's hero."

But the celebration that followed that 17-13 victory and Rose Bowl berth was anything but cynical.

"The middle-aged fan wearing the lemon and green of Oregon dashed across the artificial turf at game's end, looking for someone to hug," *Oregonian* columnist Dwight Jaynes observed that afternoon at

Parker Stadium. "There were goal posts to turn down, and there was a lot of mindless screaming to do. He would get to that. He was older than most of those down on the field—but he knew he was up to the challenge. He had been waiting too long for this chance, and he wasn't going to blow it. First, though, he looked at a stranger and shook his head. 'I can't believe it,' said the man, not at all embarrassed by the tears dribbling down his tears. 'I just can't believe it.'"

Countless Oregon fans around the state and the world felt just the same.

A QUACK HEARD 'ROUND THE WORLD

With six weeks between the Civil War and the Rose Bowl, it was time to pause and celebrate before settling into the reality of taking on undefeated Penn State. News media descended upon Eugene to tell the rags-to-riches story of the team from the Pacific Northwest with a not-very-ferocious mascot but a punishing defense called Gang Green. Fans jostled for tickets to the big game and commemorative T-shirts, soaking up the moment that hadn't come for a generation. If you had been a UO freshman the year of Oregon's last Rose Bowl appearance in 1958, you were now near retirement age.

Not only had Oregon earned its first-ever outright conference championship and its first Rose Bowl trip in 37 years, but the team's accomplishments also represented the culmination of decades of effort by countless players and coaches. The Independence Bowl trip in 1989 had been a wish come true. This was a dream.

"To me, one of the most memorable things about that time is how it was an instant transfusion of optimism in the state and on our campus," Rich Brooks remembers. "By God, Oregon *can* go to the Rose Bowl. It had gone from, 'You can't win at Oregon' and 'You can't run off-tackle against SC,' 'You can't do this and you can't do that,' to all of a sudden saying, 'It can happen.' To me it was a metamorphosis of attitude in the whole state about Oregon football. I don't think it's changed since."

To the group of Oregon seniors who had signed on with Brooks after the successful Bill Musgrave years only to see three straight seasons of disappointment, the Pac-10 championship was a validation. "We went through some tough years to get there," O'Neil says. "I think it's because of those difficult years that the '94 season in particular was special. I remember Coach Brooks saying, 'You won't appreciate this until down the road.' But those fans who had been around Oregon football for a long time probably had a better grasp of what had actually happened than the players. They knew it was a long time coming."

No wonder they called Oregon's pre-Rose Bowl pep rally in Pasadena that year "The Quack Heard 'Round the World."

THE 1995 ROSE BOWL

It was a sunny but mild afternoon in the low 70s on January 2, 1995 (the 1st being a Sunday that year, and thus reserved for pro football), in Pasadena as the Rose Bowl commenced. The eyes of the nation joined a crowd of 102,247 at the Rose Bowl for a David and Goliath matchup.

Oregon, ranked No. 12 in the Associated Press (No. 9 in the coaches' poll), had rebounded from a difficult 1-2 start with great defense and a suddenly clutch offense with the mental toughness to seize a game on the line. But the Ducks faced a Herculean task against Joe Paterno's undefeated No. 2-ranked Penn State. Led by quarterback Kerry Collins and tailback Ki-Jana Carter, the Nittany Lions were being called one of college football's all-time greatest offenses.

Oregon punted after its first possession, but things quickly got much worse.

On Penn State's first play from scrimmage, Carter burst 83 yards for a touchdown. But Rich Brooks' team weathered the storm. "After their score, we responded," says O'Neil. Indeed, just 45 seconds after the Carter play, Josh Wilcox caught a one-yard touchdown pass to even the score.

In the second quarter, a frustrating pattern developed. Oregon had consistent success moving the ball behind an offensive line led by Paul Wiggins, Bob Baldwin, Mark Gregg, and Tasi Malepeai, but failed to capitalize with points. Twice O'Neil drove the team into the red zone only to result in missed field goal attempts. At the end of the half, a drive inside the 10 fell victim to clock mismanagement. "We had called time out," Brooks remembers. "I had Danny O'Neil on the sideline and I'm saying, 'Throw it in the end zone or throw it away, because we don't have any time-outs!' He throws it short on a delay route to Cristin McLemore and the clock runs out."

Oregon fans could take stock in the fact that the Ducks were playing very competitively against what many believed to be the best team in the country (Nebraska, also undefeated, won the national championship that year in a close vote), only trailing 14-7 at halftime. Had things gone differently, the underdogs in green and gold could easily have been leading Penn State.

In the second half, Oregon continued to move the ball. Offensive coordinator Mike Bellotti, unknowingly just a few weeks away from being named head coach, devised a game plan built on screen plays and other strategies to emphasize Oregon's speed while avoiding Penn State's pass rush. "I was talking to Joe Paterno recently," Brooks says with a chuckle, "and he told me, 'I still have nightmares about that game. I've never seen so many screen passes thrown in my life!'"

Following Reggie Jordan's interception of Collins, O'Neil hit McLemore for a 17-yard touchdown to tie the score at 14 with less than five minutes left in the third quarter. Euphoric Duck fans sensed that an upset of historic proportions could actually be in the making. It was a fleeting feeling, though, as Penn State answered with a touchdown of its own just 61 seconds later on a 17-yard Carter score set up by a long kick return. One quick O'Neil interception later and Carter was back in the end zone. A tie game turned into a 14-point hole in less than three minutes.

Running back Ricky Whittle breaks for daylight against Penn State in the 1995 Rose Bowl.
Image provided by John Giustina

After that decisive period, Oregon grew more desperate by necessity, capped by an unsuccessful fourth-down attempt deep in their own territory that led to yet another Penn State score. By the time Ricky Whittle finally reached the end zone with 2:44 left in the game, it was only window dressing. Paterno's team ultimately won 38-20.

"That game was paradoxical to the rest of that year," O'Neil says. "Our team was very good at taking advantage of opportunities. In that game we got in position to score and didn't. To me that is the singular aspect of why we lost. The offense just did not score when we had those opportunities."

Still, as had been the case in their last Rose Bowl, a 10-7 loss to No. 1 Ohio State, the Ducks could hold their heads high. Oregon's offense had racked up an astonishing 501 yards. O'Neil broke or tied 13 Rose Bowl records, including new marks for pass completions and yardage. And though the defense gave up more points than usual, they had played valiantly given the often-difficult circumstances. All three second-half Penn State touchdowns, for example, had come on drives begun in Oregon territory.

Meanwhile, Duck fans weren't about to let the party end. In the 12 seasons since 1994, Oregon has posted a losing campaign only once. Capitalizing on the momentum of this storybook campaign, the Ducks established themselves as one of college football's premiere programs: a year-in, year-out winner that even the most successful previous generations of players to strap on helmets for UO had never achieved.

END OF AN ERA

After going from hot seat to hero in one season, all culminating in a Rose Bowl and a national coach of the year award, Rich Brooks was now a hot prospect. Los Angeles Rams owner Georgia Frontiere came calling, tapping Brooks to help guide the NFL team's relocation to St. Louis. His quarterback there was a familiar face: former Duck Chris Miller, whom Brooks had recruited some 12 years earlier.

Over 18 seasons on the Oregon Ducks sideline, Rich Brooks had become the team's winningest coach, although it hadn't been easy: his lifetime record was still under .500, a testament to just how many ups and downs had come in that time. It certainly didn't hurt, however, that the former Oregon State player had dominated his old team as Ducks coach, amassing 14 victories to just three losses.

Following his departure for the Rams, Autzen Stadium's playing surface was renamed Rich Brooks Field. He may have had a losing record at Oregon, but he had brought the program much-needed stability after the coaching carousel of the early 1970s. He'd also transformed a perennial loser into a winning program, and finished with a Rose Bowl season that brought grown men to shed tears of joy. If Brooks had broken Oregon fans' hearts as a player back in 1962, now he had forever captured them.

6

BELLOTTI BEGINS
1995-1998

A GREAT COACH 'STACHED AWAY

WHEN RICH BROOKS LEFT OREGON after the Rose Bowl to coach the St. Louis Rams, it didn't take the athletic department long to name his successor. Offensive coordinator Mike Bellotti's first day on the job as head coach was February 14, 1995. And how appropriate, for the time since has been a love affair. As Oregon went three years without a winning campaign before the 1994 Rose Bowl, the former UC Davis tight end had kept a relatively low profile. Bellotti wasn't quite the star coordinator that his predecessor, Bob Toledo, seemed to be, and his only head coaching experience had been at Chico State and Woodlawn High School in California. But as it happens, Oregon would be very happy with its selection.

It was Rich Brooks who took the Ducks from conference bottom-feeder to Pac-10 champion in an 18-year career in Eugene. But it has been under Robert Michael Bellotti, the even-keeled Concord, California, native with a moustache that comes and goes and a guiding sense of calm that never does, that the Oregon program has enjoyed by far its most prosperous times. When Bellotti took over, his lifetime mark based on four years at Chico State was, like Brooks at Oregon, also under .500. Yet under Bellotti, the Ducks have achieved their greatest success, including a No. 2 finish and Fiesta Bowl victory capping the 2001 season. Beyond that, Bellotti transformed Oregon's persona as much as Nike transformed its uniforms.

"Oregon is the program that changed the whole feel of the Pac-10 in the '90s," wrote Anthony Gimino of *Lindy's*. "The Ducks blazed the way for the Washington States and Stanfords and everybody else, showing that not only the big three of USC, UCLA, and Washington can become league champs and bowl game regulars."

In Bellotti's first 12 years as coach, the team has attended 10 bowl games and posted a losing record only once. No other Oregon head man, be it Len Casanova, Brooks, or even old-timers like Hugo Bezdek or Shy Huntington, has come anywhere close.

FIGUERAS SAVES OREGON...TWICE

After reaching the Rose Bowl the year before, the Oregon Ducks began their 1995 campaign with great optimism despite the departures of Brooks and graduated quarterback Danny O'Neil.

Bellotti's Ducks debuted with a tough road win against Utah 27-20, but only after incumbent quarterback Tony Graziani led the team back from a large first-half deficit. On a more dubious note, they also debuted green pants.

Oregon's home opener against Big Ten Conference foe Illinois and All-America defensive lineman Simeon Rice began just as ominously. Graziani was a late scratch from the starting lineup due to injury, giving way to unheralded Ryan Perry-Smith at quarterback, who performed admirably given his scant preparation time with the first team and led the Ducks to 27 points. Still, the Illini built a 19-point lead at one point in the game and were clinging to a 34-27 advantage late in the fourth quarter.

Then came a heroic play by Oregon safety Jaiya Figueras, who sacked the Illini quarterback, forced a fumble, and recovered in the end zone for a 34-31 win.

The next week at UCLA was the Ducks' first trip back to Pasadena since the Rose Bowl loss to Penn State just eight and a half months earlier. Led by quarterback Cade McNown, a Portland-area native, and tailback Karim Abdull-Jabbar (not to be confused with the hall of fame basketball player and former Bruin, Kareem Abdul-Jabbar), UCLA was ranked No. 12 in the AP coming into the game after trouncing Miami. But the Ducks were the better team early, amassing a 21-3 lead thanks to touchdowns by fullback A.J. Jelks, tight end Josh Wilcox, and tailback Ricky Whittle.

After trailing 24-10 at halftime, UCLA stormed back in the third quarter with a three-yard touchdown by McNown and a 52-yard scamper by running back Skip Hicks. The teams traded touchdowns after that, with Graziani keeping the ball on a seven-yard run. After UCLA tied the score at 31 with 3:52 left, Oregon marched 79 yards in eight plays for Cristin McLemore's eventual winning touchdown catch.

The Bruins weren't done, though, marching inside the five in the game's final minute. On the last play, Jaiya Figueras and cornerback Lamont Woods turned away Abdull-Jabar at the one-yard line from a touchdown as time expired. Figueras had ridden to the rescue two weeks in a row.

A TALE OF TWO HALVES

Oregon began with a jolt at Husky Stadium in 1995, with Patrick Johnson taking the opening kickoff for an 89-yard touchdown. The Ducks offense would then go on to score in three of its six first-half possessions for a surprising 24-0 halftime lead. "That kickoff return by Pat really sparked us and we got pretty fired up," UO quarterback Tony Graziani explained shortly after the game. "We wanted to come out and show them what we could do."

After racking up 273 yards in the first half (143 from McLemore), the Ducks amassed just 86 in the final 30 minutes. Behind quarterback Damon Huard (who had thrown the famous Kenny Wheaton interception the year before) and a pair of Rashaan Shehee four-yard touchdown runs, Washington stormed back to within two points. The game came down to a 36-yard field goal attempt by Husky John Wales with 1:06 left. Wales missed for the third time that day and, with no UW time-outs left, Graziani simply took a knee for a 24-22 victory.

It was Oregon's second straight win against Washington after years of losses, propelling Bellotti's team to No. 17 in the ensuing AP poll at 7-2. It also began a three-game winning streak to end the regular season with a Cotton Bowl berth.

Unfortunately, a tragic piece of history is attached to Saturday, November 4, 1995. Israeli president Yitzak Rabin was assassinated, and the announcement came to Oregon fans from radio announcer Jerry Allen during the game.

THE FEEL OF COTTON

As Mike Bellotti's first year as head coach came to a close, the team had a better record than the season prior, which had ended in a Pac-10 championship. But this time, 8-2 Oregon was knocked out of the Rose Bowl by USC, the team they'd bested in the standings last year on the final day. Still, the Ducks had plenty to play for. Beating Oregon State at home assured a Cotton Bowl invitation. They could still achieve the school's first-ever back-to-back appearances in prestigious New Year's Day bowls.

The Civil War was again a mismatch on paper, with Oregon playing its winningest stretch of football in a century of play against an Oregon State squad amidst its 25th losing season in a row at 1-9. But virtually all 46,114 in the overflow crowd knew it would be a close game. As Dan Fouts was introduced as an honorary captain and Autzen Stadium bid goodbye to a beloved class that had helped bring a Rose Bowl, the mood was electric. For the first time, Oregon also wore green pants with its home green jerseys—perhaps a successful motivating factor, though not too attractive.

Oregon State's wishbone offense continued to score few points but dominated time of possession, which combined with a stout defense under coordinator Rocky Long to keep games close. Going into the contest, Oregon's offense was the highest scoring in the Pac-10. But the Beavers kept Tony Graziani and the Oregon offense out of the end zone the entire day, taking a 10-9 lead late into the fourth quarter. But walk-on Duck kicker Joshua Smith connected from 35 yards for his fourth field goal of the day with 9:21 to play, and Gang Green held the Beavers from retaking the lead just as they'd done on that magical day in Corvallis a year before. The 12-10 victory was an ugly one in more ways than one, but the Ducks were headed to Dallas for one of college football's most historic bowl games.

DALLAS DECREE

In the Rose Bowl the year before, Oregon felt a little like a first-time Oscar nominee—excited merely to be there. This time playing on New Year's Day in a marquee bowl for the second straight season, they wanted to win. However, as important as effort and determination are in sports, it also takes the best players to win consistently. And when Oregon couldn't make a game of it against Colorado in the Cotton Bowl, the school rallied to progress the program to the next level.

Early on, Mike Bellotti's team played well, but two first-quarter drives deep into Buffaloes territory yielded only a pair of Joshua Smith field goals. And even after Colorado took the lead a minute into the second on a one-yard John Hessler run, Oregon appeared on its way to answering as quarterback Tony Graziani drove the Ducks offense inside the Buffs' five-yard line. Then everything changed: Marcus Washington intercepted Graziani's pass and raced 95 yards for a score. But that was only the beginning. By day's end, Colorado had amassed scores on each of the Ducks' five turnovers. Once leading 6-0, Mike Bellotti's team lost 38-6.

That night, the disappointed first-year head coach was at a postgame gathering with Nike co-founder and Oregon alum Phil Knight, who had run track for the Ducks in the 1950s. "What do we need to go to the next level?" Knight asked him. Bellotti told him Oregon needed an indoor practice facility and began an explanation of the long fund-raising process it would require. "No, how long would it take?" Knight interrupted, meaning from groundbreaking to finish.

"My sense was that when the football program got a little better in the mid-'90s, like so many of our alumni, he began to get more interested in what was going on," former UO vice president Dan Williams recalled years later in *The Seattle Times*. "It was around that time he began to be more interested in the university generally, and the athletic program."

In the years ahead, Oregon's facilities improved measurably, with a practice facility to complement the Len Casanova Center outside Autzen and, after the 2001 season, a major expansion to the stadium itself. After that came extravagant locker rooms and a new study center for athletes. It wasn't all thanks to Knight, but $40 million toward the Autzen expansion, for example, sure went a long way. And the commitments of Knight and other donors demonstrated that Oregon's back-to-back appearances in New Year's Day bowl games weren't a fluke, and the next time, the Ducks would be the ones in control. Funnily enough, when Bellotti's team returned to January 1 play for the 2002 Fiesta Bowl, it would be against Colorado once again—with an almost perfectly reversed score from the 1996 Cotton Bowl.

In other words, Oregon lost a battle that rainy, frustrating afternoon in Dallas, but the team was learning how to win the war.

STUMBLING WITH STUBLER

After the departure of defensive coordinator and former Dallas Cowboys star Charlie Waters when his son died tragically following the 1995 season, Mike Bellotti was already in search of his second defensive coordinator in as many years. The job went to Rich Stubler, who had been a great success in the Canadian Football League with two Grey Cup championships for teams whose defenses he guided. Stubler was considered an original defensive mind, and he favored a bold and risky formation for the Ducks defense: lining up a yard off the line of scrimmage.

It didn't work. In 1996, Oregon gave up over 32 points per game, including 55 to Washington State. The next year the defense improved slightly, surrendering 29 points a game, but that included 58 points against Stanford early in the year. A few weeks later, Stubler's off-the-ball formation was scrapped. The coordinator was soon headed out of Eugene and back to the CFL, where he would win another Grey Cup in 2000.

SALADIN'S SALAD DAYS

In the mediocre but winning years of 1996 and 1997 (with twin 6-5 regular seasons), the greatest asset to Mike Bellotti's team may have been running back Saladin McCullough. Although he's since been overshadowed by the bevy of talented rushers who have followed (Reuben Droughns, Maurice Morris, Onterrio Smith, and Jonathan Stewart), McCullough amassed over 2,100 yards in just two seasons. Against Arizona in 1996, he rushed for 223 yards on 23 carries, good for the third-most all time in one game. He really shined the next year, leading the Pac-10 in rushing on his way to breaking Bobby Moore's single-season record with 1,411 yards. "Saladin was one of the smoothest and most graceful runners I've ever seen," quarterback Akili Smith says. "His moves were just unbelievable."

PHOTO FINISH

In 1997, Oregon got off to an encouraging 3-0 start only to wind up 4-4 a month later. With the season on the line, the team traveled to Husky Stadium to face No. 4 Washington. All season, coach Mike Bellotti had been alternating his quarterbacks: Jason Maas and Akili Smith. As the No. 1-rated junior college player in America the season before, Smith was ultra-talented at both passing and running, but was taking time to learn the system under then-offensive coordinator Dirk

Koetter. Against Washington, Smith and receiver Pat Johnson rescued not only the game for Oregon, but the season as well.

With the Ducks trailing 28-24 late in the game, Smith drove the team deep inside Husky territory. "That was about the loudest I ever heard a crowd outside Eugene," he remembers. After calling time out, the quarterback huddled with Mike Bellotti and the other coaches on the sideline, but wound up diverting from their instructions once play resumed. "They told me, 'If it's man [coverage], we want you to go to Donald Haynes,'" Smith continues. "But I went against the coaches. I said, 'I'm going to Pat Johnson. That guy runs a 4.2 40.' He got the ball and that was the game winner. Amen."

Johnson didn't just get the ball—he made a spectacular diving catch, his body fully extended in mid-air like a surfboard and his fingers outstretched to just barely pull in the ball. The Huskies were left stunned, and to an extent so was Oregon. The next morning's headline in Salem's *Statesman Journal*, directly above a huge photo of Johnson's fingertip catch, exclaimed, "It Really Happened!"

VEGAS JACKPOT

Although it was a far cry from the prestigious New Year's Day bowl games the program coveted, the 1997 Las Vegas Bowl was a satisfying one for Oregon and its fans. After unprecedented success with consecutive Rose and Cotton Bowl appearances following the 1994 and '95 seasons, Oregon struggled mightily just to salvage winning records at 6-5 its next two years. Although left out of the bowl season in 1996 despite being eligible, this time Oregon found a postseason date with Air Force amidst the desert and slot machines.

The Ducks got off to their best start in any of the team's bowl games, scoring touchdowns on each of their first two offensive plays. After lining up under center for the first time at Oregon's 31-yard line

Quarterback Akili Smith. *Image provided by John Giustina*

following the opening kickoff, quarterback Akili Smith made a pointing sign with one hand before taking the ball from center—which, as it turns out, must have meant, "Go long." Smith threw a 69-yard touchdown pass down the left sideline to wide receiver Pat Johnson. The Duck defense forced Air Force to punt soon after, and Oregon had the ball back on its own 24. Next, on only the team's second offensive play and first of the drive, Saladin McCullough ran for a 76-yard touchdown.

In the second quarter, Kevin Parker recovered a blocked Falcons punt for a third touchdown, and with less than 30 seconds left in the half, quarterback Jason Maas found receiver Tony Hartley for a seven-yard touchdown. Oregon held a 26-0 advantage at halftime (thanks to two missed extra-point attempts). And while Air Force narrowed the lead during the third quarter with two touchdowns, the game ended in a 41-13 rout.

It was Oregon's first bowl game win since the 1989 Independence Bowl, but just as importantly, it was a harbinger of success to come. Over the next four years, the Oregon Ducks would enjoy the greatest run in team history with 43 wins to just 10 losses, as well as three straight bowl victories—each one on a consecutively grander stage.

RECRUITING JOEY HARRINGTON

A few days after previous Oregon quarterback John Harrington's first son was born in 1978, his former coach, Len Casanova, sent Harrington (part of Cas' last recruiting class) a letter. It was really to express Casanova's congratulations, but the correspondence on official athletic department stationery was jokingly styled as a letter expressing interest in signing the infant—one Joey Harrington. However lighthearted, Cas' letter would prove prophetic.

But the future Oregon star's official signing with the Ducks wasn't as certain as most think.

"I wasn't recruited by many schools," Joey Harrington recalls. Through the connection of a family friend at Stanford (the head of campus Catholic ministries, who delivered video tapes of Harrington's high school performances), the Cardinal became Harrington's first— or arguably his second, if you count the Cas letter—suitor.

Stanford's then-coach, Tyrone Willingham, who would go on to become the first African-American head coach at Notre Dame before moving on to Washington, liked what he saw of Harrington's heroics at Central Catholic High School in Portland. The Cardinal was ready to offer Harrington a scholarship. "The other schools—Oregon included—I was fourth or fifth down their list," the quarterback recalls. "The only reason Oregon really started recruiting me is because the other guys went elsewhere."

After Harrington threw six touchdown passes for Central Catholic in a playoff game, Washington State also entered the mix. But Harrington was turned off by the school's evasiveness. "They called me to say congratulations on the game," he remembers. "And I said, 'Well, I'm setting up my trips. I need to know if you're in or out because I need to make a decision.' They said, 'Well, we really can't make a decision at this point. We have to talk to our head coach.' They were really kind of beating around the bush, saying, 'You're really not quite good enough for us right now.'"

"The night before signing day," Harrington continues, "I was sitting in front of the mirror with an Oregon hat and a Stanford hat. You have a hard time justifying giving up a Stanford education. But the thing that my dad said was, 'Yes, you'll be able to write your own ticket if you walk out of Stanford with a degree. But if you walk out of Oregon after a successful football career, you'll be able to write your own ticket as well.'"

OPENING STATEMENT

With a talented Michigan State squad led by receiver Plaxico Burress and an ABC TV audience waiting, optimism and excitement surrounded Autzen Stadium for the Ducks' September 5, 1998, opener. Coming off the Las Vegas Bowl with Akili Smith returning, Oregon

figured to be competitive against the Spartans. What surprised everyone, though, was just how much the team dominated.

Although he improved as a quarterback throughout the previous season while sharing time with Jason Maas, Smith was now the man; his command of the game clearly had evolved. "Every year before the season starts Coach Bellotti would meet individually with all his players," Smith remembers. "Meeting with him my senior year, he said, 'Akili, you have the most talent out of all the quarterbacks here. Somehow you've got to find a way to focus on the system. And when you do, there's no stopping you.' All the time he was talking I was just nodding my head. I really committed myself." Smith also flourished under the tutelage of new offensive coordinator Jeff Tedford, the first of several NFL-bound quarterbacks at Oregon and later California to do so. "He just simplified everything," the quarterback recalls.

Although the departed Saladin McCullough had led the conference in rushing the year before, new junior college transfer Reuben Droughns was absolutely on fire against the Spartans that day, gaining 202 yards on just 17 carries, including a 75-yard beauty in the second half. "Reuben was a downhill type of back who could knock you over, and yet he still had moves," Smith adds. "He's probably the best running back I ever played with."

Complementing Droughns, Smith threw four touchdowns to four different receivers that day against Michigan State, leading Oregon to score on its first six possessions. "I thought Akili was outstanding," recalls Dan Fouts, who covered the game with Keith Jackson for ABC. "He's as fine an athlete that I've seen play in college football at quarterback." It was 34-0 at halftime and 48-0 in the fourth quarter before the benches emptied for two meaningless Spartans touchdowns. By that time, fans were already abuzz at the possibilities for the season ahead. And for the season's first five games, the future seemed limitless as Oregon put together one of the most dominating stretches in team

Running back Reuben Droughns. *Image provided by John Giustina* history. Ultimately, it also made an eight-win season feel like a missed opportunity. But on that sunny Labor Day weekend, as Smith puts it, "We stormed out of the gate."

ALIAS SMITH AND DROUGHNS

The 1998 team's Pac-10 opener against Stanford was a magical day worth savoring. A veritable runaway freight train, Reuben Droughns ran for touchdowns of 67 and 40 yards while amassing 214 yards to become the first Ducks ball carrier to break the 200-yard barrier twice in the same season. Had he not been out with an injured ankle a week earlier against San Jose State, it might have been three out of the first four games.

But Akili Smith may have been an even bigger star, throwing for four first-half touchdowns for the then-No. 20 ranked Ducks. Oregon piled up 664 yards in offense and scored its most points since a 97-0 defeat over Willamette in 1916. The 63-28 final became the most points ever given up by the Cardinal since the school began playing football in 1891.

BRUIN' A BITTER DEFEAT

Oregon traveled to Pasadena for a date with No. 2 UCLA on October 17, 1998, in a clash of unbeaten teams. It turned out tragically for the Ducks, but only after some heroic efforts. Behind quarterback Cade McNown, the Bruins jumped out 24-7 in the first half. The Ducks roared back in the second with 24 straight points of their own to take the lead behind the passing of Akili Smith, who led the NCAA in passing efficiency going into the game, and the running of Reuben Droughns, who amassed 172 yards. "The first half was my worst nightmare come true," Oregon coach Mike Bellotti told *Sports Illustrated*. "I was pleased with the way we fought back and with our effort."

Late in the fourth quarter, Oregon appeared to be driving for a possible game-winning field goal when Droughns fumbled at the UCLA

40. It was his fourth fumble of the day, but there was much worse news: he'd also broken his ankle and was lost for the season. UCLA quickly drove for a go-ahead score with McNown's 60-yard touchdown pass to Danny Farmer. The Ducks again clawed back when Smith found Damon Griffin in the end zone for a tying score with just 22 seconds left. But it was not enough, as the Ducks lost in overtime.

"It was a very emotional game," Smith recalls. "I had so many family members and friends come up to watch it from San Diego. It was like a heavyweight fight, and we were going at each other blow for blow by the end. There was no question in my mind that we had the game in hand. We just made too many mistakes."

With Droughns gone, Oregon managed to win the next week against USC thanks to Smith's heroics, including a long run straight up the middle for 50 yards and the go-ahead touchdown. Without its star tailback (replaced largely by freshman Herman Ho-Ching), though, this superlative team was now merely a good one. A blowout loss versus Arizona followed, but the biggest disappointment was a 44-41 Civil War loss in double overtime to Mike Riley's slowly improving Beaver squad. "It ended up being a tough year," Smith says, "but had that UCLA game turned out differently and Reuben not broken his ankle, we were on our way to a big bowl game—a huge bowl game."

ALOHA MEANS GOODBYE

Heading to Hawaii for an Aloha Bowl matchup against Colorado on Christmas Day in 1998, Oregon was not only looking to bounce back from a Civil War game it should have won, but also to avenge a Cotton Bowl thrashing from the Buffaloes on New Year's Day in 1996. Unfortunately, things went disastrously from the start.

Colorado cornerback Ben Kelly returned the opening kickoff 93 yards for a touchdown. Then two fumbles by Oregon freshman running back Herman Ho-Ching led to another 10 Buffalo points. Trailing 17-0, the Ducks finally got on track with an 11-yard touchdown by Darien Latimer, but the opponents from Boulder answered with a

58-yard touchdown pass just three plays later. This would be the pattern all day. Latimer again scored on Oregon's next possession, but Colorado only needed one play from scrimmage as quarterback Mike Moschetti hit Darrin Chiaverini down the sidelines for a 72-yard score.

Despite trailing 37-14, Oregon continued to fight back. Trailing 51-28 with just over 10 minutes left in the game, the Ducks scored two quick touchdowns, first on a keeper by quarterback Akili Smith and then, after Colorado fumbled, a 42-yard touchdown pass from Smith to Donald Haynes. But the 51-43 score became final when Smith was sacked and then threw three straight incompletions.

It was an unfortunate end to a 1998 season that, despite an impressive 8-4 record, felt like a missed opportunity. In the regular season, only Arizona (which finished 12-1) had beaten Oregon soundly, while losses to UCLA and Oregon State had slipped away in overtime. And had talented tailback Reuben Droughns not broken his leg in Pasadena, the team seemed destined for a major New Year's Day bowl instead of the lower-tier Aloha Bowl.

But amidst the disappointment, coach Mike Bellotti and his team had reason for optimism. The Oregon Ducks were about to enter their most successful three-year run in team history—one that would ultimately bring talk of a Heisman Trophy and even a national championship.

KNIGHT AND SHINY ARMOR

The 1999 season brought a new look for Oregon football. Although it wasn't the first time the team had changed its jerseys, pants, and helmets (that process had been ongoing since the team's beginning in 1894), the redesigned Duck uniform that Nike unveiled was an outright reinvention.

Gone was the interlocking UO logo, replaced with a single O shaped symbolically like the Autzen Stadium oval (pre-renovation) on the outside and the Hayward Field track on the inside. The green and yellow colors got darker and brighter, respectively, with a yellow stripe extending down the jersey sides and pants that, along with Nike's redesign for the NFL's Denver Broncos, ushered in a new style frequently copied afterward. The green helmets featured a then-unique metallic finish that refracted light. It was inspired, Nike designer Todd Van Horne said, by the plumage of actual mallards. The uniforms also took advantage of new fibers and materials, becoming more streamlined and hugging a player's pads. In conceptual drawings, the Oregon players looked more like superheroes than footballers.

Many of the alumni were skeptical, but the uniforms were a smash hit with Oregon's players and incoming recruits. "You should see how much time these guys spend looking in the mirror in the locker room," coach Mike Bellotti told Portland's *Willamette Week*. And with recruiting becoming an ever more ruthless, high-stakes campaign, Oregon was looking for every advantage it could find against schools like USC, with countless blue-chip players in its backyard.

The new uniforms also emphasized the role of Nike CEO Phil Knight in the Ducks' program. In the years ahead, not only would the team's fortunes improve on the field, but from the snazzy uniforms to an expanded Autzen Stadium to futuristic and luxurious new locker rooms, it seemed at times like they were the Nike Ducks as much as the Oregon Ducks. Any cynicism, though, had to be weighed against the fact that Knight's benefaction was unequivocally helping the cause of Oregon football. Maybe plasma screens in the locker room or bold uniforms couldn't win games, but they could help attract the players who would do just that. Like Nike itself, Oregon was now becoming a brand. And while the Ducks lacked a storybook history on par with that of Notre Dame, Alabama, or Southern California, a spirit of youthful innovation and dare sent the message that Oregon's time was now.

Just as Knight and Nike's fingerprint on Oregon seemed to be growing exponentially, though, a major rift came. In late April of 2000, the Ducks coming off a successful 9-3 season capped by a comeback Sun Bowl win and a promising future with Joey Harrington at quarterback, Knight abruptly withdrew all financial support for

Oregon—including some $30 million that had been expected for the expansion of Autzen. The reason? The university had joined the Worker Rights Consortium, a watchdog group critical of Nike's treatment of employees in Indonesia and Southeast Asia. Knight felt betrayed. The university was torn by different allegiances within the school. Students and faculty had largely driven the WRC alliance, while the athletic department and fans sweated over losing their golden goose.

Ultimately, Knight and Oregon made up. The school pulled out of the WRC and joined a more Nike-favorable worker oversight organization, to the accusations of copout by some and the tremendous relief of others. That fall, Knight began attending games again, and soon the Autzen expansion plan was back on. As it turned out, the brouhaha was merely an aberration in a burgeoning Knight-Nike-Oregon relationship. "Phil is so identifiable with the school and the school is identifiable with Nike," says Dan Fouts. "The contributions he has made to the university over the years—and not just athletically—have been important to the school and the state."

But the WRC incident has not been forgotten, either. After suffering for much of the 1970s and '80s and never a real powerhouse throughout its history, Oregon was transforming into a giant of college football—but not on its own, which has been both to the program's benefit and, perhaps, its peril.

7

CAPTAIN COMEBACK'S ADVENTURES
1999-2001

HARRINGTON VS. FEELEY

WITH AKILI SMITH having graduated to the NFL as the Cincinnati Bengals' sixth pick in the draft, redshirt sophomore Joey Harrington and junior A.J. Feeley were the top two candidates for the starting quarterback position in 1999. And with a very tough season opener at Michigan State looming, the Ducks would need whichever young signal caller was placed in the starter's role to perform well from the beginning.

Throughout fall camp, Feeley and Harrington battled to a virtual draw. Harrington had a quick release and strong leadership qualities. "I remember Joey used to play quarterback of the scout team his freshman year," Akili Smith recalls. "A lot of the time he would just burn up our first-team defense. He'd be throwing fireballs out there. People were talking about him pretty much from the get-go. We knew he was going to be great." However, Feeley possessed a bigger body and excellent passing skills. As it happened, both quarterbacks would one day start in the NFL.

"A.J. and I both played very well during fall camp," Harrington remembers. "It was a very close, tough thing to call, which the coach told both of us. The original plan was that A.J. was going to start, but I was going to take a few snaps. At that Michigan State game we would split it a little bit, just because nothing was fully decided. But then he went out and threw for about 340 yards, and there was never really a good time to take him out of the game. And so he won it—he won it on the field. You can't take the guy out when he's playing so well. So for four games, he was one of the top 10 passers in the country."

Oregon lost its season opener 27-20 to the Spartans in East Lansing, Michigan, but Feeley played well. He continued as the starter (spelled occasionally by Harrington) in blowouts against Texas-El Paso and Nevada. Against USC that year, Feeley and Harrington shared credit in a triple-overtime classic. But Feeley injured a nerve in his elbow against Washington in a 34-20 road loss. It didn't immediately require the quarterback to lose playing time, but after another tough road loss, 34-29 to UCLA, the starting job became more vulnerable again. "I could tell he was in pain," Keenan Howry remembers. "But before that, A.J. was tearing it up. If he had stayed healthy, there's no telling what would have happened, because we were on a roll. But Joey ended up making the most of the opportunity."

The next week at Arizona, Harrington relieved Feeley and rallied the team to a 44-41 comeback win. The following Saturday at Autzen, Harrington did it again, driving Oregon to a winning score in the final two minutes against Arizona State. The "Captain Comeback" legend was born and Joey Harrington would never relinquish his starting job.

"I got lucky in the sense that he got a little bit dinged up," Harrington muses of his battle with Feeley for the starting job. "But I don't think I would have been in that position had the competition not been so close coming out of camp. As a 21-year-old college kid, Coach tells you you're going to get a chance to play and then you don't see the field for five games, you get a little frustrated. But, you know, that was just a matter of waiting."

HEATING UP AT CENTURY'S END

After finishing the season with five straight victories under new starting quarterback Joey Harrington, the Ducks traveled to El Paso to play Minnesota in Oregon's first Sun Bowl appearance since 1963. It was the last day of the 20th Century, and some were fearful the Y2K computer-dating crisis would bring society to a standstill. But Oregon fans still came to support their Ducks, part of a total Sun Bowl crowd just over 48,000.

The game didn't start well for Oregon, as the Golden Gophers' eighth-ranked defense held the Ducks scoreless in the first quarter. Luckily, the Ducks' defense, led by Peter Sirmon's 16 tackles, was just as stingy. After a 7-7 halftime deadlock, Oregon took the lead on Harrington's second touchdown keeper of the day. A Nathan Villegas field goal made it 17-13 at third quarter's end. But the lead only lasted one play into the fourth, as a Gophers touchdown reclaimed the advantage for coach Glen Mason's team.

Harrington was already becoming known for his late-game heroics, and with 7:28 remaining he lined up under center for what would be Oregon's longest scoring drive of the 1999 season. Beginning from their own 13, the Ducks marched 87 yards in 12 plays, including a dramatic fourth-down pass from Harrington to receiver Tony Hartley for 23 yards. "We were so winded," receiver Keenan Howry remembers. "I was bent over sucking air after one play ended on that drive, and Tony came up to me and yelled, 'Man, stand up!'"

Yet it was the fatigued Howry who caught the winning 10-yard touchdown with 1:23 left on a "load pass right" play from Harrington.

Going into fall camp as a freshman that year, Howry hadn't even expected to play much—until fate intervened. First, fellow freshman receiver Sammie Parker was injured in practice and forced to redshirt. Then the starting receiver's job unexpectedly came up for grabs when Bobby Nero was declared academically ineligible. "I'd worn No. 15 in high school, but Bobby had it, so I had to settle for 88," Howry remembers. "We're out there about the third day of two-a-day practices,

and [receivers] coach [Chris] Petersen tosses me the No. 15 jersey. He said, 'You want it?' I felt bad, but I had to take it." (In 2006, Petersen led Boise State to a stunning Fiesta Bowl upset against Oklahoma.) By Oregon's third game in 1999, a 72-10 thrashing of Nevada, Howry was not only starting but was already becoming the Ducks' go-to receiver.

On the winning Sun Bowl play against Minnesota, Howry realized before the ball was snapped that no defender was covering him. "I kept trying to get Joey's attention," he says. "When the play starts I run down the field looking back like Joey's going to throw it to me, but we had a play-fake in the backfield and he hadn't seen me yet. So I just ran my corner route like I was supposed to. I'm waving my hands because still nobody's on me. Then I could see Joey's eyes get super big, and he threw it. But it was a horrible pass. I could tell he was just so excited and he didn't want to overthrow it, so he actually threw it behind me and low as I'm running away from it. I had to stop and slide and catch the ball on my back hip. I roll over and the ref's saying touchdown."

Minnesota had time to answer, however, especially given college football's temporary clock stops after first downs. That's when Oregon's defense saved the day. Dietrich Moore sacked quarterback Billy Cockerham and forced a fumble, which Saul Patu recovered to seal the victory. And with it, Harrington and the Ducks began a streak of three straight bowl wins, each one more prestigious, for the first time in Oregon history.

"I really didn't play that great for a lot of the game," says Harrington of the 1999 Sun Bowl. "But you get into a groove at the right time and go down the field and score a touchdown with a minute and a half left in the game, and all of a sudden it's something that people remember."

TRIPLE PLAY

The 2000 Ducks opened Pac-10 play at 2-1, but were only beginning to hit their stride. The team had produced easy wins over overmatched

Receiver and kick returner Keenan Howry. *Image provided by Eric Evans Photography* opponents Nevada and Idaho, but lost between in a squeaker 27-23 at Wisconsin. Now, though, the real test came: the beginning of Pac-10 Conference play against No. 6 UCLA. With ESPN's "College GameDay" broadcast live outside Autzen Stadium before the game (broadcaster Lee Corso picked Oregon and put on the Duck-head mascot) and an ABC telecast of the contest hosted by Keith Jackson, Oregon faced a strong opponent with millions watching.

The game was a battle for the line of scrimmage by two teams seeking to establish the run, the Bruins for running back DeSean Foster and Oregon for junior college transfer Maurice Morris.

In the off-season, Oregon had battled USC all the way to signing day for Morris' services. Hailing from a South Carolina family with 15 children, Morris was quiet but an agile workhorse on the field.

"I picked up Mo at the airport in Portland before the season and he came over to my parents' house for dinner, but I don't know that he said 10 words," Joey Harrington recalls. "The portions he took from the dinner table were very small. After all, if you're one of 15 kids, you need to save some for your brothers and sisters. He spoke only when he was asked a question. Every response was, 'Yes sir,' 'No sir' or 'Yes m'am,' 'No m'am.' But the more you got to know him, he turned out to be a bit of a joker. He was the guy who nobody ever expected, which I think played into his hands."

Against UCLA, the Ducks gained the upper hand thanks in large part to Morris' 139 yards and two touchdowns on 37 carries. "He had kind of an awkward running style. It almost looked like he had a bit of a limp," Harrington adds. "But when he hit the corner, oh God—look out!" The biggest heroes of the game, though, were Oregon's defensive players. They hassled quarterback Ryan McCann all day, stuffing Foster and bringing their safeties to the line to blitz passes. Thanks to a bevy of quarterback sacks, UCLA finished with minus-nine yards on the ground. The 29-10 win lifted unranked Oregon into the Associated Press poll at No. 20.

"Barely seven days before, UCLA was campaigning for the No. 1 ranking and boldly talking about a national championship," wrote Ken Goe in *The Oregonian*. "Saturday, UCLA was not even the best team at Autzen Stadium."

A week later, the nation's new No. 6-ranked team, Rick Neuheisel's Washington Huskies, came to Autzen Stadium, again with an ABC television audience. (Neuheisel was ostracized by Oregon fans even more than most Husky coaches since his Colorado team had run up the score against UO in the 1996 Cotton Bowl.) Joey Harrington found Justin Peelle for the game's opening touchdown, but Oregon was again most effective on the ground, earning 229 yards. A 17-3 halftime lead became 23-3 early in the third quarter on Joey Harrington's one-yard keeper shortly after a bomb to Keenan Howry brought the Ducks to the seven-yard line. Bound for the Rose Bowl that year, Washington climbed back to within seven points late in the game, but Duck defender Matt Smith batted down quarterback Marques Tuiasosopo's final attempt. The 23-16 final made for Oregon's fifth win over the Huskies in the past seven years. "They came out and they were barking in the tunnel," Ducks defensive lineman Jason Nikolao said after the game, "but we turned those big dawgs into little puppies."

After a week off, No. 9-ranked Oregon traveled to the Los Angeles Memorial Coliseum to face quarterback Carson Palmer and USC. The Trojans took a 7-0 lead on their opening drive, but Oregon soon equaled with a Harrington-to-Morris touchdown pass. In the second quarter Harrington found Josh Line for a 23-yard score, and not long after halftime hit receiver LaCorey Collins in the end zone from 14 yards out. Winner of the Heisman Trophy two years later, Palmer brought USC back within four at 21-17, but a Harrington touchdown pass to tight end Justin Peelle sealed this victory. It was Oregon's fourth win in five years against USC.

MIRACLE IN THE DESERT

For all the remarkable comeback wins that marked the Joey Harrington era at Oregon, perhaps none can surpass the 2000 marathon in Tempe, Arizona, between the Ducks and Arizona State.

The final box score is eerily even: Each team scored one touchdown in the first quarter, two in the second, one in the third, and three in the fourth. In reality, though, Oregon trailed most of the game. First, the Ducks fell behind 21-7 in the second quarter, until Joey Harrington brought the team back with touchdown passes to Keenan Howry and Marshaun Tucker.

Then, in the fourth quarter, Arizona State seemed to have the game in hand with a 49-35 lead. That's when Harrington found Tucker for a 32-yard score. Still, Oregon remained a touchdown behind. On ABC's television broadcast, the Ducks' quarterback could be seen pacing the sidelines and shouting to his teammates, "We are not gonna lose! We are not gonna lose!"

Oregon got the ball back, but seemed to come up just short when a fourth-down pass to Justin Peelle was stopped at the one-yard line. "I threw Justin a little stick route from the six-yard line going in," Harrington recalls. "I was expecting to get single coverage on the backside receiver. But they played a cover two, which dictated that I go to Justin. He ran a great route and got open and I put the ball there. But as he turned, the linebacker clipped his back heel, and Justin stumbled just enough where he didn't have enough power to get to the goal line. We were walking off the field and I'm thinking, 'How did that happen? We just lost the game.' All that ranting and raving on the sidelines, and we were going to lose."

With less than two minutes left and Oregon without a timeout, all ASU had to do was gain a single first down to run the clock out. And on third down, as quarterback Jeff Krohn handed off to Devils tailback Mike Williams, who scooted past the first-down marker, they seemed to do just that.

Something unusual must have been happening in the stars those few days. The game took place just before Halloween, shortly followed by the controversial presidential election between George W. Bush and Al Gore. For in what became a fateful play, ASU's Williams, a freshman, fumbled just inches after gaining the game-clinching first down. Linebacker Michael Callier hit him from behind and cornerback Jermaine Hanspard recovered at the 17-yard line with 27 seconds left. Given new life, Harrington found Justin Peelle on the next play in the corner of the end zone for the tying touchdown.

Ironically, given the 49-49 score and 42 combined fourth-quarter points, both teams failed to score in the first overtime. The second time around, Oregon drove for a touchdown by reserve running back Allan Amundson. Once again, ASU answered with a touchdown of its own. But wait! After lining up for the extra point attempt, the Sun Devils ran a fake. Normally not the holder on kicks, Krohn caught the snap and rolled to his right before lofting a pass toward tight end Todd Heap. Oregon safety Rasuli Webster was there, however, to break up Krohn's pass in the end zone. And like that, Oregon had won: 56-55. "It takes a few lucky bounces," Harrington says. "It also takes a group that's ready to take advantage of it."

HOLIDAY HEALS WAR WOUNDS

The eight-game win streak that Oregon produced in 2000 had only happened one previous time in school history: in the 1933 campaign headed by coach Prink Callison, including victories over Linfield, Gonzaga, and Columbia. But this time around, the Ducks felt the bitter disappointment of a season-ending loss on the road against Oregon State.

The Beavers enjoyed their best season in school history in 2000. Led by quarterback Jonathan Smith, running back Ken Simonton, and receiver Chad Johnson, OSU defeated Oregon 23-13 in the only Civil War ever to feature both teams ranked in the top 10 of both major polls. Coach Dennis Erickson's team jumped to an early 14-0 lead and held on, thanks in large part to three Joey Harrington interceptions and three fumbles amidst a ferocious Beaver pass rush led by Nick Barnett. After beating Oregon, the Beavers blew out Notre Dame in the Fiesta Bowl.

Although the Ducks were part of a three-way tie for the Pac-10 championship, they were the only team to miss out on a marquee Bowl Championship Series bid. Washington had lost to Oregon earlier in the year, but their victory over OSU and undefeated non-conference record gave Rick Neuheisel's team the Rose Bowl bid.

Meanwhile, Oregon would have to settle for the Holiday Bowl in San Diego, commonly referred to as the premier non-New Year's Day postseason game. Ironically, the opponent was tougher than those UW and OSU faced in their more prestigious postseason contests: a Texas squad led by much-hyped young quarterback prodigy Chris Simms, son of New York Giants star Phil Simms, as well as freshman receiving sensation Roy Williams.

The Holiday Bowl had a long history of games decided in the final moments, and this one was no different. The Ducks took command initially, driving twice for touchdowns in the first quarter: first a one-yard score by Justin Peelle, then an incredible trick play to the end zone in which receiver Keenan Howry threw an 18-yard strike to Harrington, all alone but struggling to keep his balance as he stumbled and dove to the goal. "We'd been running that play in practice all week but we didn't get it right until the last day," Howry recalls. "When they called it in the game I was kind of shocked. Then I got the ball and I couldn't even see Joey—the linemen were blocking my view. I just threw it toward the corner. Then he was stumbling so much I thought, 'Oh man, he's never going to get there in time.' On the sidelines we were joking about it afterward: Is Joey an athlete? Can't he even run? But he found a way to make that catch and get it to the end zone."

Running back Maurice Morris. *Image provided by Eric Evans Photography*

Texas bounced back after Harrington's TD catch, though—and then some. After driving for two scores to tie the game, the Longhorns took a sudden lead thanks to Greg Brown's 23-yard interception return for a touchdown and 21-14 advantage at intermission.

Mike Bellotti's team went right back to work, however, with a 55-yard screen pass for a touchdown by Maurice Morris less than four minutes into the third quarter. Drives by both teams ended without points until under 10 minutes remained in the game, when Harrington ran nine yards for the end zone. Oregon's quarterback had now run, passed, and received for three different touchdowns. And the glory of that achievement lasted all of 18 seconds in game time: the Longhorns' Victor Ike ran the ensuing kickoff 93 yards for a score to once again equalize the contest.

It was at times like this Oregon was lucky to have Captain Comeback on its side. Four minutes after Ike's dagger, the Ducks' Jason Willis crossed the goal line. As ESPN announcer Mike Terico exclaimed, "Oregon leads!" And the enthusiasm was prophetic: This would turn out to be the winning touchdown—but just barely.

Simms guided the Longhorns within striking range multiple times in the last five minutes, including a last-minute try made possible by an Oregon fumble. The Ducks also deliberately scored for Texas on a safety to give themselves more punting room, which almost backfired as Simms took just a couple of plays to get Texas back inside the Oregon 30. Diminutive but virtuosic Oregon cornerback Rashad Bauman, however, thwarted Texas' tall, speedy receivers time after time. A cousin of much-beloved former Duck defender Kenny Wheaton, Bauman had suffered painful cramps throughout the second half, stretching with trainers on the sidelines whenever Oregon's offense was on the field. But he was there at the end, saving the game and letting Texas know about it with a wall-to-wall smile and several trash-talking verbal volleys.

When the clock finally hit zero, Mike Bellotti's team had squeaked by for a 35-30 victory before 63,278 and a nationwide TV audience. It wasn't happening on New Year's Day, but it felt sufficiently redemptive. The victory also gave Oregon its first top-10 finish and 10-win season in its history—against one of college football's most storied teams. "This was such a milestone for the program," Oregon cornerback Rashad Bauman said. "They're a good team and a good program, but we were playing a team, not tradition."

In years past, this would be the apex of an era for Oregon. But this Duck squad was just getting warmed up. Virtually every key player was coming back for 2001, and would be joined by another NFL-caliber tailback to complement Morris. For the first time in school history, there was legitimate reason to believe the almost unthinkable—a Heisman trophy for Harrington, or even a national championship for the Oregon Ducks—could be within reach.

COACHING FOR COOKIES

Because part of a quarterback's job is to act like a surrogate coach on the field, players at that position often end up forming tight bonds with members of the staff. By his senior year, not only had Joey Harrington flourished under Jeff Tedford as Akili Smith and A.J. Feeley had. But Harrington also enjoyed a familial attachment, as many players have, with other longtime assistants such as Neal Zoumboukos, Nick Aliotti, Gary Campbell, and Don Pellum. "That's the great thing about the staff," says Harrington today. "I can walk back into the building and I'll still know three quarters of them. They're just great guys. Don Pellum, I remember he would always hover around the front desk when we got our mail anytime he saw a box for me, because my mom would send me cookies. He knew I'd be opening the box of cookies, and he'd be hovering there, he'd be waiting."

Other times, the interaction was more serious. "There were a couple times when we had to put in freshmen or walk-on offensive linemen, and I was a bit nervous." Harrington explains. "Jeff Austin hadn't played a down my junior year when he started for us at center. I remember saying to Coach Zoum…'Are you sure about this?' And he said, 'Don't even think twice. Jeff is going to be ready to play.' And wouldn't you know it, Jeff played his butt off. With very few exceptions, when we were there, Oregon never got the big recruits. We were all guys that other schools had passed on—especially the offensive linemen. But Coach Zoum had a way of getting guys to play. I always felt comfortable because I knew they were going to be ready."

THE BILLBOARD

With its first team ever to finish in the top 10 mostly coming back, optimism about the 2001 season was sky high. The Pac-10 media picked Oregon to win the conference crown, but the team's biggest hype was self-generated.

Kicking off a Heisman Trophy campaign for Joey Harrington, the athletic department used donor funds to erect a huge billboard in New York City across from Madison Square Garden. The senior quarterback was shown standing in his green Ducks home uniform, helmet in hand, against a white background. The 100-foot billboard's headline had Harrington's last name playfully crossed out and replaced to read "Joey Heisman." National media attacked the ploy as a heavy-handed escalation of college football campaigning, but it was easy for a bunch of writers in New York and Los Angeles to say so—they weren't struggling to get noticed far away from the nation's populated centers and sacred gridiron grounds. As with the uniforms, Oregon knew it couldn't win just competing the old way—the Ducks had to stand out. What the campaign lacked in subtlety, it made up in bravado.

EVERYTHING AND NOTHING AT STAKE

After the hype of Harrington's billboard, it was time to go to work. And seventh-ranked Oregon could not ease into the season with No. 23 Wisconsin coming to Eugene. An early 10-0 lead, punctuated by Harrington's 23-yard touchdown pass to Justin Peelle, was cut to 10-7 at

Running back Onterrio Smith. *Image provided by John Giustina*

halftime, which outlined the pattern all day: Oregon jumped ahead, Wisconsin answered, and vice versa. The Badgers' starting quarterback, Brooks Bollinger, was a late scratch for the game with a bruised liver, but his backup, Jim Sorgi, turned out even better.

Still, the game was ultimately another feather in the cap of Captain Comeback, as Harrington directed a nine-play, 78-yard drive for the winning score on his own quarterback keeper. No. 3 in the green jersey hoisted his arms into the air while still stuck in the pile of blockers and tacklers. "He played pretty good," Bellotti told *USA Today*. "Not as good as he is capable of, but he made some plays by looking off some receivers and hitting the open man."

However, there was now another co-star in Oregon's ensemble cast: running back Onterrio Smith, who had transferred from Tennessee after a marijuana charge got him kicked off the team. In a new one-two running punch with the established Maurice Morris, Smith dazzled. Later that year against Washington State, he would break Oregon's single-game rushing record. Personality-wise, the individuals were polar opposites. Whereas Morris was quiet and reserved, "You couldn't get Onterrio to be quiet," Harrington laughs. "But he was always smiling, always laughing. The two complemented each other so well."

A week later, Oregon racked up a sloppy 24-10 win against Utah. But before the team played another game, the terrorist attacks in New York, Washington, and Pennsylvania on September 11, 2001, brought the nation to a halt. Overnight, the state of the world seemed to change. As rescuers searched the debris of the World Trade Center, the Pentagon, and United Airlines flight 93, all college and pro football games were cancelled. By September 22, though, the nation yearned for the normalcy and diversion of watching football again, meaning Mike Bellotti had to get his team back to thinking about Xs and Os amid all the sobering distractions.

"It really was surreal," the Oregon quarterback remembers. "I remember standing out on the practice field during that week, and they had shut down the airports so there were no airplanes. But we're close enough to the coast that you could see the military planes going by, protecting the coast. We would hear those jets flying by. You don't realize it until you have all the airplanes taken out of the sky how often you hear them. I remember we were all standing out there on the practice field and heard that lone jet go by, and everybody just froze and kind of watched it."

As Oregon met USC at Autzen Stadium that evening, the national anthem, preceded by a moment of silence, took on exponentially greater meaning. But there was a game to play—and what a game it was. Like the Arizona State barnburner the year before, the Ducks unquestionably seemed to have the game lost only to pull out a near-miracle.

Oregon jumped out to an early lead thanks to a trick play in which Onterrio Smith took Harrington's pitch and threw to a wide-open Justin Peelle for a 35-yard score. Another Smith, Ducks defensive back Steve Smith (no relation), returned a Carson Palmer pass for a touchdown—one of his three interceptions that night to tie the Autzen record. But Oregon's 21-6 lead quickly evaporated into a 22-21 deficit thanks to two long touchdown receptions by USC's Sultan McCullough (Saladin's younger brother, who nearly signed with Oregon) and Kareem Kelly.

The Ducks appeared to miss their comeback chance when backup kicker David Rosenberg's 43-yard field goal attempt with 1:20 remaining was partially blocked by 6-foot-4 Trojan lineman Bobby DeMars. But USC couldn't run out the clock. Particularly crucial was a third-down play in which Palmer instinctively threw the ball out of bounds to avoid being sacked, thereby stopping the clock. The 56 seconds were just enough for Oregon's offense to drive within field goal range. This time, the kicker was freshman Jared Siegel at 32 yards out with 12 seconds left—and he made it, to the cathartic, astonished screams of 45,765.

"We knew when we got the ball back...we'd do it," Peelle told UO student newspaper, *The Daily Emerald.* "I wish we could do it earlier and stop with this crap, but we'll take it. We've just done it so many times and have that swagger, that confidence in ourselves."

YOU ONLY LOSE ONCE

When Florida State lost in Tallahassee on October 13 (the same day Oregon defeated Cal 48-7 in Berkeley), the Ducks became proud owners of the nation's longest home winning streak at 23 games. But it would only last a few days. Behind coach Tyrone Willingham, for whom Harrington had almost played, Stanford stole one at Autzen Stadium 49-42, thanks to a couple of well-timed fluke plays, including a blocked punt and an onside kick, which would ultimately prove the difference maker in keeping Oregon out of that year's national championship game.

OREGON'S TURN TO FIESTA

The Ducks faced added pressure going into the annual season-ending Civil War game against Oregon State. At 9-1 with a No. 5 ranking, they were still alive for a berth in the Bowl Championship Series national championship game that year, the Rose Bowl. Also at stake was the chance to avenge last year's stinging 23-13 loss in Corvallis, which had cost Oregon an outright conference championship and a trip to Pasadena. But as Joey Harrington came down the tunnel to the Autzen Stadium field, he paused for another reason.

"I didn't want to come out because I knew it would be the last time playing there," Harrington remembers. "It was sad, because I didn't want it to end." The game would also be a swan song for seniors like Maurice Morris and Rashad Bauman, both of whom starred for Oregon that day.

The game was played two weeks later than normal in order to accommodate a nationwide broadcast on ABC. And it was clear winter had arrived. It didn't just rain at the 2001 Civil War. It was a monsoon. Water deluged the field as if the gods had suddenly awoken, and the skies turned an incredible turquoise color, particularly in the wild second half.

The Beavers were a year removed from trouncing Notre Dame in the Fiesta Bowl and their No. 4 ranking in the final AP poll of 2000. Quarterback Jonathan Smith and running back Ken Simonton had returned for their senior years, but the season had soured for the Beavers. At 5-5, they were looking to beat Oregon to salvage a winning record and bowl game. Simonton was also looking to become only the NCAA's fifth player to rush for four straight 1,000-yard seasons.

Defenses dominated the first half, with the Ducks and Beavers trading field goals for a 6-3 OSU lead at intermission, which stuck throughout a scoreless third quarter. But the tension was mounting, and sooner or later a big play seemed destined to break.

Shortly after the fourth quarter began, it did, in the form of an electrifying 76-yard punt return for a touchdown by junior Keenan Howry. The team's blocks, particularly one by Ty Tomlin, had opened a tremendous hole right in the middle of the field, and after cutting inside Howry scampered to the end zone without being touched, giving Oregon a 10-6 lead.

"All game long their punter had been kicking low, line-drive punts," Keenan Howry remembers. "Coach was telling me, 'He's been punting bad all game. If you get a chance, you might get an opportunity for a big return here. And we need it.' So I trot out there on fourth down and I mark off my line. Coach told me to scoot up a little bit. The next thing I know the ball gets punted, I get up under it, catch it, and as I look down the field I see a guy coming at me. But at the same time I saw one of my guys [Tomlin] was about to make a block on his right side. So I kind of made a little move, hopped to the right, and I saw this big, huge lane. I just took it straight up the middle, and there was nobody there. After the first five yards, I'm looking around thinking maybe the whistle blew or something. But I just kept running, and the next thing I know I'm in the end zone and my teammates are all there."

Emboldened by the dramatic score, the defense quickly forced Oregon State to punt again, and this time the Ducks' offense marched downfield for another score, with Morris dragging a horde of Beaver defenders over the goal line for a 17-6 advantage. But Oregon State roared back as Smith hit Josh Hawkins for a 24-yard touchdown with 2:05 left. A successful two-point conversion brought the Beavers within three.

Then, as Oregon's offense tried to kill the clock, Harrington fumbled on a third-and-nine play while trying to scramble away from defensive lineman Kyle Rosselle, who punched the ball free. Linebacker James Allen recovered at the Ducks' 33 with 1:38 left.

"We were standing on the sidelines," Harrington remembers of a timeout before the play, "and Bellotti told me, 'Run 24 Load, but just keep it. Don't tell anybody.' As I faked it I could see the running back was like, 'What the…?' I turned the corner and there's a defensive end waiting there for me. In hindsight, I should have just dove straight to the turf. But I tried to kill some time, and he knocked that ball out. God, if my heart didn't stop. I thought for the second year in a row Oregon State had ruined our season. That would have just been too much."

But in a play that recalled Kenny Wheaton's famous game-saving interception against Washington in 1994, Rashad Bauman picked off Smith and saved the game for Oregon, which could now kill the clock with a 17-14 advantage—and a major sigh of relief. "Rashad, God bless 'em," Harrington says today with a sigh.

It wasn't pretty, but the Ducks had a Civil War win. Unfortunately, the closeness of the game kept Oregon out of the BCS championship, and Harrington's Heisman Trophy chances were hurt by an 11-of-22 passing performance.

"I don't care about that," the quarterback says today. "The thing that made me the most upset was that stupid computer, saying we didn't beat our in-state rival by enough in a monsoon in December, and because of that we don't get to go to the national championship game. That was ridiculous."

But Oregon's mood would improve considerably after their next game, a 38-16 whipping of Colorado in the Fiesta Bowl.

FOURTH-QUARTER SUPERMAN

Joey Harrington finished his career as arguably the most accomplished football player in Oregon Ducks history, leading the team to a No. 2 ranking his senior year, a 25-3 overall record as a starter, and three straight bowl wins while becoming the school's first Heisman Trophy finalist. But more than anything, Harrington will be remembered for his comebacks. Ten different times he led Oregon from behind in fourth-quarter play.

"He was high-strung and high-energy, always ready to go," Keenan Howry recalls. "My parents used to always joke around and say that Joey had ADD [Attention Deficit Disorder] and he needed some Ritalin. You'd see him on the sidelines and he'd be jumping around and really raring to go. But the thing was, when he got on that field he was calm. When the pressure went up, he was even-keeled and kept us going."

Early in games, though, Harrington was often quite mortal. "I remember my senior year we were at home and it was the third quarter and we were in a bit of a funk," the quarterback says today with a smile. "Bellotti came up to me and said, 'You know, you don't have to wait until the fourth quarter to start playing.'"

Time and time again in his two and a half seasons as Oregon's starter, Harrington would look very human only to come to the Ducks' rescue as Superman. How did he do it?

"First and foremost is luck," Harrington says. "But a little bit of luck brings success, and success brings confidence. So more than anything, I was just confident. It wasn't as if I walked into that situation and automatically had that confidence, but we'd gotten a couple breaks along the way, which made us think, 'You know what? We can do it.' I honestly believe there's nothing more important in that situation than everybody having confidence it can happen. You're not worried about forcing the issue, or having to make the play, because you know it's going to happen."

Oftentimes by necessity, he admits, the confidence has to be an act. "Sometimes I was scared to death," he adds. "But you'd never get me to admit it. Part of playing that role, part of being the quarterback, is convincing the 10 other guys that you know what's going on—even if you've got no clue—because if they don't look at you and see complete confidence, they will doubt themselves. And the only way that you're going to get anything done is for them to all believe, and for them all to believe in you. So there were plenty of times when I faked it. I can think of two separate occasions offhand where we went on to win, but at one point I thought, 'You know what? It's done. We've lost.' But you have to convince everyone else you're not thinking that, even though the natural human reaction is to think that."

NO. 2 TO NONE

Although Oregon had risen after the Civil War victory to a No. 2 ranking in both the Associated Press and the ESPN/*USA Today* coaches' polls on December 9, the Bowl Championship Series ranked them differently, weighing computer polls into a convoluted formula nobody seemed to think was fair. As a result, Nebraska claimed a spot in that year's national championship game, the Rose Bowl, against undefeated No. 1-ranked Miami, even though the Cornhuskers had been trounced by Colorado in their last game and hadn't won their conference championship.

And it was Colorado that Oregon wound up playing in the Fiesta Bowl instead. As outraged as Duck fans, players, and coaches had a right to be, this game in the desert would become the greatest day in Oregon football history.

Despite going into the game ranked at No. 3 behind Oregon, Colorado's dominating performance over Nebraska and the strength of a bruising running game had made them the toast of bowl season. It was fashionable to call them the best team in the country. "I wouldn't be surprised if Colorado scores 50 on Oregon," ESPN commentator Lee Corso said during TV coverage before the game.

After each team punted on its initial series, Colorado was indeed the first to take the lead. Facing third-and-nine at midfield, quarterback Bobby Pesavento barely avoided a bevy of Duck defenders to find running back Cortlen Johnson on a screen pass, going all the way to the Oregon 19-yard line. The Buffs soon broke through for a touchdown.

But Oregon quickly answered back. Joey Harrington began with an emphatic 35-yard completion to Sammie Parker that set the tone for the drive and showed Colorado they weren't going to stampede away with the game. After Parker's completion, Harrington found Jason Willis for a 20-yard gain. The next play, a pass to Keenan Howry from the Colorado 28, ABC broadcaster Brent Musburger (a Portland native) described as follows: "Joey...fires—got it, touchdown! Let the fireworks begin." After one quarter the score was tied at seven, but the momentum seemed to favor the team from Eugene. "We'd been giving Joey a hard time all year for under-throwing it to us," Keenan Howry remembers. "But in that game he was just laying it out there for us perfectly."

In the second quarter, defensive coordinator Nick Aliotti's squad began to do what few thought they were capable of: The team shut down the Buffaloes' vaunted rushing attack. Meanwhile, the offense continued to hit its stride. In a play that is now a Ducks classic, Harrington found Sammie Parker on a deep post pattern and lofted the ball to him perfectly in stride. Parker easily outran his defender for the goal line in a spectacular 79-yard touchdown. "He's in a foot race—they won't catch him," Musburger exclaimed. It was Harrington's longest pass play of the year.

The touchdown brought Oregon's first lead of the game, but the No. 2 Ducks were just getting started. Next it was running back Onterrio Smith's turn as he caught Harrington's shovel pass at the six-yard line for a score. At halftime, it wasn't shocking to see Oregon

ahead. But what may have surprised even the Ducks themselves was just how much they were dominating. ESPN's Mel Kiper wrote that the game was over at 14-7 when Harrington threw the bomb to Parker. "He looked one step ahead of everyone the whole game," Kiper said of the Ducks' signal caller.

Despite a relatively comfortable 21-7 halftime lead, Mike Bellotti's team didn't let up. In fact, Oregon was the only team to score in the third quarter—in spectacular fashion at that. With the ball at the 49-yard line, Maurice Morris took a handoff from Harrington and appeared to be down at the 21-yard line as he momentarily lay on his back atop another player. But Morris' body had never touched the ground, and he simply rolled off the Colorado defender, regained his footing, and scampered the rest of the way towards the goal line. It would have made any all-time Ducks highlight reel, even in a regular-season game. To happen in the Fiesta Bowl on New Year's Day—with 74,118 fans in the audience and a TV audience of approximately 40 million—was magical. Kiper may have been exaggerating when he called the game over at 14-7, but after Morris' touchdown and a 28-7 lead heading into the fourth quarter, some viewers could be forgiven for beginning the celebration.

When Colorado kicked a field goal with 5:47 to go, it ended a scoreless span of over 45 game minutes. By that time, it was 38-10, Oregon having added a Justin Peelle touchdown and Jared Siegel field goal. After Colorado's first-quarter touchdown, the Ducks had put up 38 straight points. Prominent players got the credit, but linemen like Jim Adams, Ryan Schmid, Dan Weaver, and Joey Forster had also led the way.

Going into the Fiesta Bowl, Oregon's defense had been the greatest area of concern. But Duck defensive players like linebackers Kevin Mitchell and Rasuli Webster, lineman Junior Siavii, and cornerbacks

---

Quarterback and Heisman Trophy finalist Joey Harrington compiled a 25-3 record as starter. *Image provided by Eric Evans Photography*

Steve Smith and Rashad Bauman used speed and agility to completely smother the Buffaloes' ground game. In a pass-first situation as Colorado was forced to play catch-up, Pesavento's throwing led to three interceptions by Oregon's Steve Smith. For Nick Aliotti, the subject of criticism in years past when Oregon defenses didn't perform, it was an utter vindication. "Pleaaase," Colorado safety Robbie Robinson told *Sports Illustrated*'s John Donovan after the game, "there's no comparison. [Oregon] is a far better team than Nebraska."

The team effort included spectacular play from a host of players. Yet no one could argue that John Joseph Harrington was the MVP of the Fiesta Bowl. The front page of *The Eugene Register-Guard* the next day displayed a giant photo of Harrington with his arms raised above his head, forming his hands into the shape of an 'O.'

Harrington didn't win a national championship, as *Sports Illustrated* had suggested was at stake in a cover story earlier that year featuring Oregon's quarterback and OSU tailback Ken Simonton (each pictured with a sword, impaling a stuffed toy of the other team's mascot). Harrington never played in a Rose Bowl. He came close to winning the Heisman, but lost to an almost instantly forgotten Nebraska quarterback, Eric Crouch. Harrington often experienced periods of mediocrity in his Oregon career only to come alive with the game on the line, as if almost bored without the extra jolt of adrenaline. He was also a bit of a pretty boy by testosterone-heavy football standards: the quarterback played piano and his teammates good naturedly nicknamed him "Princess." But from the time he took over the starting position midseason as a sophomore until his last snap in the Fiesta Bowl, Joey Harrington's Ducks team was consistently the best squad in Oregon's century-plus play.

Harrington lost just three times as a starter: a 27-23 squeaker at Wisconsin in 2000, a tough 10-point game on the road that same year versus Oregon State's best team ever (Dennis Erickson's Fiesta Bowl winner), and a blown lead against Stanford in 2001. The remaining 26 games were all victories. Before the Fiesta Bowl broadcast was complete, Musberger openly questioned whether the Heisman balloting would have turned out differently had the vote come directly after this game.

At the same time, even Harrington wasn't bigger than Oregon at this moment. As an orange sunset gave way to darkness over Tempe, Arizona, the Duck players and coaches—newly outfitted in the customary championship T-shirts and baseball caps—took turns hoisting the Fiesta Bowl trophy. Oregon was the undisputed Pac-10 Conference champion, had defeated the country's hottest team in a Bowl Championship Series game on New Year's Day, had won 11 games for the first time in its history, and was guaranteed to finish no lower than No. 2 in the Associated Press poll. (The ESPN/*USA Today* coaches' poll was contractually obligated to vote the loser of the national championship game No. 2.)

In fact, the excitement of Oregon's Fiesta Bowl achievement was augmented even more with the knowledge that, should Nebraska upset Miami in the Rose Bowl, Oregon would likely share the national championship with the Cornhuskers. "Who's No. 1?" stated the banner headline on the aforementioned *Register-Guard* cover. As we now know, Nebraska wound up getting trounced, and the national title went to the Hurricanes. Oregon undeniably should have been in that Rose Bowl against Miami instead of Nebraska. But because the Fiesta Bowl had been such a fairy tale, the whole affair went down a lot easier—like having foie gras instead of caviar, or a Porsche instead of a Ferrari. And beating Miami would have been a Herculean task.

"I don't think you could have drawn it up any better than what happened," Harrington says. "Yeah, it would have been great to play for a national championship. Would we have won that game? Nobody will ever know. Would we have been heavy, heavy underdogs? Yes. That was a team that has put 10 guys into the NFL in the first round, six from that season, including D.J. Williams, Jonathan Vilma, Jeremy Shockey, Clinton Portis. It's full of NFL Pro Bowl players. It would have been a heck of a game for us. And a more incredible story had we won it. But if I was to write something, if I was to sit down and write that season, I don't think you could have written it any better."

8

EXPANDING DREAMS
2002-Present

AUTZEN ANEW

WITHIN DAYS of Oregon's 2001 Civil War victory, construction crews hurried to work with the almost unheard-of task of expanding a major stadium in less than nine months—before the next season's opener. The team, led by architect Ellerbe Becket and Hunt, the general contractor, fashioned much of the materials for the expansion off-site, including a series of Y-shaped columns that would comprise Autzen's iconic new entrance.

The architects faced two possibilities for the expansion: add an upper deck of seats, which was more common in stadium design, or maintain the architectural integrity of Autzen's original seating bowl. They chose the latter. By expanding on just one side, the symmetry of the old Skidmore, Owings, and Merrill design of 1967 was lost, but Ellerbe Becket won the job in part because it was the only firm that proposed in its master plan an as-yet-unbuilt future expansion of the other side, which could someday increase Autzen's seating to 70,000.

Some students and faculty carped about the millions being spent on a football team's home. With 54,000-plus presently buying up game tickets, though, the Oregon athletic department was self-sufficient, completing a long journey from the economic woes that had compounded the dark days of the 1970s. Like the famous line from the movie *Field of Dreams*, Autzen's expansion proved "if you build it, they will come."

CLEMENS AND THE QB CADRE

The state of Oregon is not traditionally known for producing high numbers of Division I college football players, but in the fall of 2001 a trio of quarterbacks emerged as premiere talents: Kellen Clemens of Burns, Derrick Anderson of Scappoose, and Nic Costa of Aloha. Clemens, a rancher's son as comfortable on horseback as in an automobile, was the most mobile of the three, while Anderson stood tall with a strong arm. Coming from the Portland area instead of small towns like the other two, Costa had aced the toughest competition. Which would the Ducks set their sights on, and would they get their man?

"I wanted to go to Oregon the whole time," Clemens remembers. "I talked to Coach Bellotti and said, 'This is the place where I'd like to come.' He hadn't offered any quarterback a scholarship yet."

That fall the trio of quarterbacks competed at a Nike-sponsored camp in Eugene, which also included Michael Harrington, Joey's younger brother. It was here that Oregon decided on Clemens. Bellotti called Clemens a week after the camp and offered the scholarship. When Anderson signed with Oregon State, the two were forever paired as rivals.

MIDSEASON PEAK

The 2002 Ducks seemed destined for great things. Gone were graduated heroes of the Fiesta Bowl team such as Harrington and Morris, but skill players like Keenan Howry and Onterrio Smith remained. And new quarterback Jason Fife started the season hot

Quarterback Jason Fife jumps for the end zone against Michigan in 2003.
Image provided by Eric Evans Photography

enough to make Duck fans temporarily forget his immortal predecessor. In the team's first five games, each a victory, all but one included winning margins of over three touchdowns.

Heading to Pasadena to play 25th-ranked UCLA, though, No. 7 Oregon faced a much sterner test. Bruins quarterback Corey Paus would throw touchdown passes of 59, 71, and 53 yards in a 316-yard overall day. But three of his passes were also intercepted, including two by maligned freshman cornerback Aaron Gipson.

Although Fife was 14 of 18 for 202 yards, including touchdown passes to tight end George Wrighster and Keenan Howry, the latter on a dramatic 74-yard scoring play, the Ducks relied on their running game. Junior tailback Onterrio Smith established a new school record with his sixth consecutive 100-yard rushing game.

For the second year in a row, though, the game came down to a field goal attempt. And, as in the previous year's 21-20 squeaker, UCLA missed. This time, the attempt was affected by the Oregon defense, which held the Bruin offense on third down to force a longer attempt. Earlier that day, Duck kicker Jared Siegel had hit a school-record 59-yard field goal attempt.

Oregon was now 6-0 and ranked sixth in the nation, but it was almost all downhill from there. With Smith injured and Fife's hot streak cooling, Mike Bellotti's team would lose five of its last six regular-season games, including an embarrassing 45-25 defeat to Oregon State, followed by a depressing Seattle Bowl loss in the rain to Wake Forest at Seahawks Stadium in which Clemens took most of the snaps.

CLEMENS VS. FIFE

Several times in his coaching tenure at Oregon, Mike Bellotti has defied conventional wisdom in rotating two young men at the quarterback position. Most coaches and other football experts believe it's best to decide on one player, supporting him through the inevitable ups and downs of learning the toughest position on the field. Bellotti has often drawn a different conclusion: that competition brings out the best in both players, and pushes one to ultimately assume the full-time starter's role. In 1997, it was Akili Smith and Jason Maas sharing time. In 1999, it was Joey Harrington and A.J. Feeley. In 2006, it would be Dennis Dixon and Brady Leaf. And in 2002 and 2003, it was junior Jason Fife and sophomore Kellen Clemens.

Fife tutored under Joey Harrington during the Holiday and Fiesta Bowl seasons and initially held the starter's job as a junior in 2002. But Clemens was the blue-chip recruit waiting in the wings, his cowboy persona and unlimited potential exciting fans. Fife started out red-hot in 2002 when Oregon began 6-0, but as that record ultimately fell to 7-6, Clemens began to see playing time.

"I think it was definitely the best way to go, just because that's the way that we went," Clemens says diplomatically. "Sharing time is difficult, though. As a quarterback, there's only one of us on the field and you want to be the guy who goes out there. But having the chance to learn from Jason in the younger years of my career was definitely a help. In the role that he and I were in, he was very good about it and very helpful. There's a lot of guys who would be in that position sharing the spot after starting the year before who wouldn't have handled it as well as he did. He did a very good job of helping me along and being a good teammate."

Still, while the rotating of quarterbacks may have helped Clemens, it cost Fife. "I don't think the coaching staff ever put their complete faith in Jason," Howry says. "Even when A.J. and Joey had been competing, the coaches treated it like A.J.'s team once he won the job. Then, for three years, it was Joey's team. But then, instead of putting their faith in Jason, they made it Onterrio's team. We weren't attacking anymore. And then when Onterrio got hurt, suddenly we were lost."

HELLO HALOTI

When Oregon announced the signing of Salt Lake City defensive lineman Haloti Ngata on national letter-of-intent day (the first Wednesday in February), it was a coup the Ducks had rarely enjoyed:

the successful recruitment of one of the most coveted players in America was covered by most every sports media outlet. Only a few recent players, such as Jonathan Stewart and Cameron Colvin, have wrought equal signing-day hype. Ngata was actually listed as the top high school defensive prospect in America. Coming from a devout Mormon family, he seemed to be a lock for BYU. When he chose Oregon instead, Mike Bellotti had a 6-foot-4, 308-pound (338 by the time he left) difference maker.

Ngata didn't take any time to make an impact. Even as a freshman in 2002, he made running the ball against Oregon an altogether more difficult proposition. Against UCLA that year, Ngata's block of a Bruin extra point was the difference in a 31-30 win. Ngata, paired with fellow defensive lineman Igor Olshansky, who in training could bench press more than any player ever to strap on a helmet in Eugene, caused an Oregon team traditionally anchored by its offensive stars to suddenly put its "Big Uglies" (to borrow announcer Keith Jackson's term) on billboard advertisements.

As colossal a presence as Haloti Ngata was at Oregon, his tenure was far from easy. During his freshman year, his father passed away. In the season opener at Mississippi State in 2003, he suffered a season-ending knee injury. Ngata ultimately decided to forgo his senior season at Oregon in part to help pay medical bills for his mother, who was suffering from kidney failure. Tragically, in January of 2006 she too passed away. If Ngata hung his head, though, it would never be in relation to his performance on the football field. It's fitting that the 'g' in his last name is silent, pronounced "nada"—which is exactly the punishing message he delivered to opposing offenses.

HAIL TO THE VICTORS INDEED

Arguably no regular-season game stands as a prouder moment than the Ducks' 2003 victory over Michigan. And with the weather a perfectly sunny 62 degrees, a full house of more than 58,000, and a nationwide televised viewing audience on ABC, the setting could not have been more ideal.

"One of the big guys has pitched camp here in the Willamette Valley of Oregon," announcer Keith Jackson said in his broadcast intro. "The Michigan Wolverines [are] coming to a place they have never been to play a team that has feasted on such moments of opportunity. They are the Oregon Ducks, a feisty flock whose habitat includes one of the loudest college football stadiums anywhere."

Michigan entered the game with significant hype, ranked No. 5 in the ESPN/*USA Today* coaches' poll with a 3-0 record, including a victory the week before against Notre Dame. On ABC's pregame broadcast, studio host John Saunders picked the Wolverines to play in the national championship. Tailback Chris Perry was also a Heisman Trophy contender, leading the nation in rushing and scoring.

At 3-0 with a No. 22 ranking of their own, the Ducks weren't exactly easy prey themselves. Kellen Clemens led the Ducks on an impressive 69-yard opening drive, but on third and goal at the one-yard line, his apparent quarterback sneak touchdown was marked short of the goal line. "That is clearly a touchdown," commentator Dan Fouts told the viewing audience. Worse yet, the ensuing field goal attempt was blocked and returned for a touchdown by the Wolverines' Jeremy Leseur. After Michigan's missed extra-point attempt, Oregon found itself losing 6-0 despite having the ball for all nine minutes of elapsed game time.

But the second quarter belonged to the Ducks. First, Terrence Whitehead ran for a 19-yard touchdown, going virtually untouched on a trap up the middle behind senior center Dan Weaver (a former walk-on and younger brother of former Ducks tight end Jed Weaver). It was the first touchdown surrendered by the Wolverines in a first half that season and the first time that Oregon had ever scored on Michigan.

Lloyd Carr's team desperately clung to its run-first strategy despite getting virtually nowhere. Then, when Michigan tried a fake punt, it bounced off one of their blockers and Oregon recovered at midfield.

Defensive lineman Devan Long. *Image courtesy of Erik Bishoff*

Jason Fife was temporarily under center in Mike Bellotti's two-quarterback system, charged with running the no-huddle offense. Fife finished the quick-marching drive on an option keeper, faking to Whitehead and scampering 15 yards past the goal line. A picture from this play would grace the next week's cover of *Sports Illustrated* with the headline, "Dazzling Ducks: Rich, Cool, and 4-0 (Quack Quack)."

After another fruitless Michigan possession capped by Devan Long's sack of John Navarre, the dam appeared to burst. With 7:50 left in the second quarter, Steven Moore returned Michigan's punt 61 yards for another touchdown. The 21-6 score held until halftime.

In the second half, Clemens led Oregon to its largest advantage, 24-6, with a third-quarter Jared Siegel field goal. But Michigan was finally beginning to throw the ball, and an apparent rout became a close football game as Navarre connected with Jason Avant for a touchdown with 4:03 in the third.

Clemens was again relieved by Fife and a surging no-huddle offense, led by linemen Nick Steitz, Mike DeLaGrange, Adam Snyder, Joey Forster, and Dan Weaver. But Whitehead was stopped at the Michigan five on third and goal to end the quarter. Worse yet, Oregon was turned back on a fake field goal attempt, giving up the chance to extend the lead to two touchdowns and handing the momentum back to its opponents.

Navarre and his receivers didn't waste time as Steve Breaston scored from 10 yards out and Braylon Edwards gained a two-point conversion, narrowing the gap to 24-21. In the first half, Oregon had outgained Michigan by 187 yards. At this point in the second half, however, the Ducks were 28 yards behind. They were, as Jackson said, "trying to save what has been a valiant effort, and what at times seemed astounding."

Then came what could be called Oregon's game-winning play: Keith Lewis blocked Adam Finley's punt, and true freshman Jordan Carey recovered the ball in the end zone.

An interception by Justin Phinissee ended Michigan's ensuing drive, prompting another of Jackson's folksy aphorisms: "He got in front of Breaston and lo and behold, 'Look what I found, Mama!'" The Wolverines eventually struck back, making the score 31-27 on Braylon Edwards' touchdown and taking the ball back on an onsides kick. But Oregon's defense held, the Wolverines' chances ending on fourth down as a pass bounced off Edwards' fingertips.

"I think the key was never giving up," Mike Bellotti told reporters afterward. "I have great respect for Michigan, but I'm very proud of my Ducks today."

Michigan coach Lloyd Carr was even more effusive about Oregon and its home-field advantage. "Autzen's 59,000 strong make the Big House [Michigan's 105,000-seat stadium] collectively sound like a pathetic whimper," he told the *Michigan Daily*. "It's louder than 'The Swamp' at Florida, 'The Shoe' in Columbus, and 'Death Valley' at Louisiana State. Autzen Stadium is where great teams go to die."

LIGHTS OUT, CLEMENS IN

Kellen Clemens had a difficult start in Oregon's night game against Cal in 2003. After completing just one of six passes for 14 yards in the first half, he was benched in favor of Jason Fife.

But when Fife also struggled and Cal stretched its 10-7 halftime lead to 17-7 with Aaron Rogers' third-quarter touchdown pass, Mike Bellotti decided to give Clemens another chance. First, though, Autzen Stadium technicians had some game saving of their own to do after the lights went out early in the fourth quarter. The game was halted for 20 minutes and Cal (now led by former Oregon assistant Jeff Tedford) even went to the locker room.

After the lights came back on, Clemens himself seemed to have been rebooted along with the power system. He went 8-for-12 for 103 yards in the final quarter, leading Oregon to a dramatic come-from-behind win with two long drives capped with a 31-yard touchdown pass to tight end Tim Day and a go-ahead score by tailback Terrence Whitehead.

"That was the turning point for my career at Oregon," Clemens recalls. "We were kind of on the brink as a team going into that game. How good were we going to be? We had lost a couple, so it was a big turnaround for us as a team and for me, I know, as a quarterback. I think it did something for my confidence, but I also think it boosted my teammates' confidence in me." Clemens' Harrington-like comeback also helped cement him as the Ducks' quarterback and ended the rotation with Fife.

But the win was still sealed by defense. With less than a minute to go, Rogers drove Cal to Oregon's 33-yard line and time to spare for three attempted touchdown throws. The last one was caught—but by Oregon safety Keith Lewis for a game-saving interception with four seconds to go.

The win would propel Oregon to a Sun Bowl appearance against Minnesota, in which Oregon played well but came up one point short, 31-30, when the game-winning field attempt was no good. "We were low on wide receivers," Clemens remembers. "Jason Fife was actually our fourth wide receiver. But Sammie Parker set the Sun Bowl record for catches and tied it for touchdowns. He just played his tail end off. It was a lot of fun to go out and play. Unfortunately, we just wound up on the wrong side of it."

The bowl-win drought since the Fiesta Bowl was now at three seasons, two games and counting, but Oregon once again seemed headed in the right direction. Besides, with Fife now graduated, Clemens was indisputably the man.

IMPLOSION

In Oregon's debut against Indiana in 2004, Kenny Washington ran the opening kickoff 100 yards for a touchdown, but the play was called back on a penalty. And the mistakes were only beginning. On the offense's opening drive following the flag, Kellen Clemens fumbled, leading to a Hoosier field goal. There would be seven Oregon turnovers overall (three by Terrence Whitehead alone), resulting in a 23-0 halftime deficit. In the second half, Oregon rallied back to within 30-24 (Indiana's lone touchdown coming on a kick return), but two Clemens interceptions inside the Indiana 20 in the last five minutes sealed the Ducks' fate. By game's end, Oregon had outgained the Hoosiers in total yards by a wide margin: 495-198. But the victory was elusive.

And that's pretty much what happened to Oregon all season: one step forward, at least one step back. 2004 has been the only year under Mike Bellotti in which the team has finished with a losing record, 5-6. In the middle of the season, the team won four in a row, but suffered three close losses at year's end, including a 28-27 heartbreaker against Cal that saw a potential winning score stopped just short. To the Ducks' credit, the 5-6 record could easily have been 7-4. And indeed, this team would prove its mettle a year later.

SENIOR CHEMISTRY CLASS

In 2005 Oregon's seniors swore there would be no more losing. On defense, cornerbacks Aaron Gipson and Justin Phinissee, both of whom had struggled as freshman starters three years earlier, began shutting down cornerbacks, while All-American Haloti Ngata continued to dominate line play. On the other side of the ball, once offensive coordinator Andy Ludwig departed for Utah, Bellotti turned to former BYU head coach Gary Crowton to install a spread offense that would put the ball in the hands of its skill players more often. The spread also gave Clemens, now a senior quarterback with superb passing and leadership skills, a chance to flourish by providing him more on-field responsibility. But the spread was only as good as its players and their ability to work together. Luckily, that came naturally to the trio of Clemens, receiver Demetrius Williams, and running back Terrence Whitehead.

"A lot of times Demetrius and I changed plays without saying or signaling anything," the quarterback remembers. "We'd just look at each other and know what the other was thinking. I had that same relationship with Terrence. A lot of times you change things in the middle of a series, but Terrence and I would change things in the middle of a play."

Whitehead had not been as highly touted a running back as recent predecessors like Maurice Morris and Onterrio Smith, but his consistency helped keep Oregon from losing momentum that year, even as Clemens was lost for the last four games of the season. "He was hurt every week, but he never played hurt," Clemens adds. "That's one of the reasons I think he snuck up on people in the record books. He didn't have those huge games, but he didn't have tiny games either. He was just Mr. Consistent."

Against Fresno State, Whitehead made one of the most impressive plays of his career. With four minutes left and Oregon clinging to a narrow three-point lead, Whitehead took a seemingly routine short pass at the Bulldog 42 and proceeded to zigzag his way through or

Running back Terrence Whitehead. *Image courtesy of Erik Bishoff*

around seemingly every player on the field en route to what would become the game-winning touchdown in a close 37-34 victory for then-unranked Oregon over No. 23-ranked Fresno State. "That last touchdown put it in the bag," Clemens says, "and that was all Terrence."

BROKEN BUT NOT BEATEN

It wasn't supposed to be like this—not again. Memories of 1988, when a dazzling Bill Musgrave-led squad began the year 6-1 only to lose its final five games after the quarterback's season-ending broken collarbone, were all too vivid for the Ducks on the evening of October 22, 2005, against the Arizona Wildcats in Tucson.

Oregon was back to its winning ways in 2005 with a 7-1 record behind senior quarterback Kellen Clemens, its only loss to a No. 1-ranked Southern California with two Heisman winners in quarterback Matt Leinart and running back Reggie Bush. A team that had lost at home to Indiana just a year ago seemed poised to match the regular-season record of the legendary Joey Harrington-led Ducks of 2001.

Then, in an instant against Arizona, the dream appeared to die. With eight minutes to go in the game, Arizona's Copeland Bryan sacked Clemens. The quarterback knew instantly that it was a serious injury, and the X-rays would reveal a broken ankle. By the time he was assisted off the field, Clemens had already begun contemplating. "I thought maybe my career was over," he recalls, "not just my career at Oregon, but football in general."

There was no time to stop and ponder, even for Clemens. Untested Dennis Dixon had to be inserted into the game after scarcely a warm-up snap. This was no pressure-free case of mop-up duty for the redshirt sophomore, a former four-star recruit. Dixon could run and pass with equal ability: a potential Michael Vick in the making, but skinny and yet to develop that level of polish in his game.

Dixon lasted just a few plays before being knocked unconscious, out for at least the remainder of the game. Next up was Brady Leaf, younger brother of former Washington State quarterback Ryan Leaf, who took the Cougs to the 1998 Rose Bowl but suffered a quick, high-profile flame-out in the NFL. Brady, like Ryan, was a more traditional pocket passer and not as athletically skilled as Dixon. But to a shell-shocked Oregon team, he had poise.

Clemens had initially been carted into the locker room for doctors to attend to his broken leg, but the injured signal caller insisted on being escorted back onto the sideline in order to guide whichever quarterback was on the field.

Yet it was a defensive play that allowed Oregon to salvage a come-from-behind win. With 2:46 to go in the game, linebacker Brent Haberly returned a Mike Bell fumble 34 yards for a go-ahead touchdown. "I was going to put a hit on him, and then I saw the ball," Haberly told the Associated Press after the game. "My eyes lit up, and I grabbed it."

Oregon's moxie in overcoming adversity against the Wildcats showed that, however painful the Clemens loss was, the team needn't give up on the season. After all, they had become bowl eligible two wins ago. There was much to play for.

In the weeks ahead, Oregon would will itself to a 3-0 record, securing wins over Washington State, California (in overtime), and Oregon State, the last by a blowout 55-10 score at Autzen Stadium in fog so thick the TV announcers had trouble naming players. (It also masked Oregon's latest uniforms.) The team's only post-Clemens loss came in a Holiday Bowl squeaker to Oklahoma, a loss the Ducks would avenge 10 months later.

Had Clemens never been injured, perhaps the BCS wouldn't have shied away from a 10-1 team without its star, as they did with the Dixon and Leaf-led team. Oregon fans felt more than a little slighted when teams with lesser records like Notre Dame scooted past the Ducks into coveted New Year's Day games. But then again, Oregon's historic 2005 season has now become that much more impressive for the adversity overcome along the way.

BEATING...OKLAHOMA!

In an unlikely twist of scheduling fate, Oregon wound up playing the Oklahoma Sooners in three consecutive seasons from 2004-2006. The series didn't start well for the green and gold, but it finished with a bang.

Oklahoma had won the first of these three matchups easily in Norman in 2004, the year Oregon finished 5-6—not a good time to be facing freshman running back sensation Adrian Peterson. In the 2005

Receiver Demetrius Williams. *Image courtesy of Erik Bishoff*

Holiday Bowl, the vastly improved Ducks sought revenge, flushed with the confidence of a 10-1 regular season. But Oregon came up just short. Trailing 17-14 in the game's final moments, Brady Leaf (who had shared playing time with Dennis Dixon ever since Kellen Clemens' injury) led the Ducks downfield for a potential game-winning touchdown, or at least a tying field goal. But Oklahoma linebacker Clint Engram intercepted Leaf's pass at the 10-yard line with 33 seconds left, preserving the Sooner victory.

So when Bob Stoops' team came to Eugene on September 16, 2006, for the second half of the regular-season home-and-home series, the chip on Oregon's shoulder had doubled in size.

The 18th-ranked Ducks and 15th-ranked Sooners each came into the game at 2-0. By this time, junior starting quarterback Dennis Dixon seemed to have distanced himself from Brady Leaf and occupied the majority of playing time. Oregon sophomore Jonathan Stewart was beginning to show why he'd been the top-rated high school running back in the nation. He'd amassed 168 yards on just 22 carries in the opener against Stanford for a gaudy 7.6-yard average before being held out for all but one play (which happened to be a touchdown) with a sprained ankle the next week against Fresno State. Amazingly, backup tailback Jeremiah Johnson's average was even higher: 7.9 per carry. And the play of wide receiver Jaison Williams had abruptly ended a preseason of worries as to who would step up following the graduation of NFL-bound Demetrius Williams.

With a raucous overflow crowd of 59,269 cheering them on, the Ducks took a 7-0 first-quarter lead on Stewart's two-yard touchdown and built a 13-3 advantage by halftime. But Oklahoma roared back in the second half, outscoring Oregon 14-0 in the third quarter to take a 17-13 lead thanks to Malcolm Kelly's 31-yard touchdown reception from quarterback Paul Thompson. Sooners tailback Adrian Peterson, held relatively in check during the first half, was also starting to heat up in a big way. He would finish with 211 yards on 34 carries.

In the fourth period, the game became a shootout. Oregon tied the score at 20 on a 30-yard touchdown pass from Dixon to Williams, only to see Oklahoma answer with a Peterson touchdown followed by two field goals. By now Peterson was dominating, bursting for double-digit yards with regularity and moving the chains to keep the ball away from the Ducks. With less than two minutes to go in the game, Oregon trailed by 13 points. But the offense got its groove back just in time.

A Dixon touchdown from 16 yards out made it 33-27 with 1:11 left. But Oregon's only hope was to get the ball back on an onsides kick.

And in one of the most controversial plays in all of college football that season, they did just that. Kicker Luke Bellotti, the head coach's son, bounced a squib kick off the Autzen Stadium turf, where a blur of Sooners and Ducks piled on the ball. After the whistle blew and officials began to pull away players, an Oklahoma player seemed to have the ball. But the referee ruled in favor of Oregon—he had seen a Ducks player down with possession before being stripped. This was the first season of instant replay in college football, and further review affirmed the call on the field: Ducks' ball.

The game was telecast on ABC, and commentators Dan Fouts and Tim Brando both argued that possession should have belonged to the Sooners since an Oregon player had touched the ball illegally before it traveled the necessary 10 yards. But in reality, the call could have gone either way. The distance traveled toward the goal line was a difference of millimeters; had the referee initially ruled for Oklahoma on the field, that call may too have withstood the scrutiny of a booth replay, which asks for "indisputable video evidence" in order to overturn a call. No matter how much criticizing would be done after the game by both analysts and Sooner fans, nothing was indisputable about the play.

There was still action to be settled on the field after the onsides kick. With only 46 seconds left, Dixon found Brian Paysinger for a 23-yard touchdown. The Autzen Stadium crowd went bonkers, but Oklahoma had one last chance. And they took quick advantage, as Reggie Smith returned a squib kick to the Oregon 27. After the euphoria of just a few moments earlier, Duck fans turned silent with the threat of heartbreak as Oklahoma lined up for a field-goal try as time expired. But this fairy tale of a game would have a happy ending. Sooner kicker Garrett Hartley's 44-yard field goal attempt was blocked.

Unfortunately for Mike Bellotti's team, the elation of this historic victory would be relatively short-lived. The next week, Oregon looked every bit a contender for the Pac-10 championship and a prestigious bowl game with an impressive 48-13 blowout on the road against Arizona State. But then the Ducks were cut down 45-24 against Cal, beginning a dismal six losses in the team's last nine games, including three straight to end the regular season and an embarrassing 38-8 Las Vegas Bowl loss to Brigham Young.

Still, the Oklahoma win seemed to symbolize just how far the Oregon Ducks had come in 114 years of play. With superlative facilities, a fervent fan base, and a host of world-class athletes to go with almost annual bowl appearances, the team in green and gold once counted as a college football bottom feeder in the 1970s was now able to routinely compete with the nation's most storied football programs.

Unquestionably, there have always been and will continue to be difficulties along the way, for Oregon lacks the prominence and homegrown recruiting pool that many of its competitors enjoy. But as pandemonium ensued at Autzen Stadium as the clock struck zero and fans poured onto the field that sunny September afternoon in 2006, there was reason for optimism beyond the predictions and predilections of any one season.

Oregon's football program stands today on the shoulders of giants, boasting players like Van Brocklin, Renfro, Fouts, Moore, Musgrave, Wheaton, O'Neil, Smith, Droughns, Harrington, Morris, Bauman, Howry, Clemens, and Stewart, along with coaches such as Bellotti, Brooks, Frei, Casanova, and Huntington. What keeps Autzen sold out, what accounts for Duck merchandise seen all over Oregon and beyond, and what has more blue-chip recruits committing to Eugene than ever before, though, isn't the past. It's the future.

"They are one of the premier athletic programs in the country now," Dan Fouts says. "That's a great tribute to the men in charge: [athletic director] Bill Moos, and before him, Bill Byrne, did a great job of making sure that the facilities were upgraded. And being able to keep a coach like Mike Bellotti has been huge. I hear nothing but good things about the University of Oregon when I travel around the country."

Way back in 1894, Oregon's first coach was so eager to get the team on the field he scheduled the first game half a year early. As the Ducks and their followers look ahead, that irrepressible spirit remains. And it's not just their archrival Beavers and Huskies that might want to watch their backs, but the Wolverines and Fighting Irish, the Trojans and Gators, and the Buckeyes. The Oregon Ducks have had their ups and downs over the decades, but today it doesn't take an instant replay to see they're ready to soar.

Epilogue

LIFETIME DUCK

IT WAS NOVEMBER 15, 1980: my first Civil War game, age eight. My mom's boss had given her two choice 50-yard line tickets in the Oregon State donor section at Parker Stadium, gladly handed over to my dad. In my excitement the morning of the game, I forgot to bring a coat despite near-freezing temperatures. I shivered for three hours, taking turns with my dad using his coat. But happily so, because Oregon quarterback Reggie Ogburn ran and passed his team to a lopsided 40-21 victory. Eventually, though, the surrounding Beaver season-ticket holders began to tire of my bratty taunts. A woman behind us hit me on the head with her orange and black pompon. A man one row ahead turned around to say, "Little kid, I hope you freeze to death." And indeed, I came down with a heavy fever and flu that night. But it was worth it: I was madly in love with the Oregon Ducks.

Growing up in McMinnville, a small Oregon farm town less than an hour's drive from Corvallis, being a Duck fan was hazardous. More than once I succumbed to playground fisticuffs born from Civil War animosities, which only fueled my fervor all the more. Besides, after the doldrums of losing throughout most of the 1970s, the Oregon Ducks were beginning a slow climb to prosperity that would last throughout my childhood and continues today, some 27 years after my first time at Autzen (a 7-7 tie with Kansas, also in 1980).

In junior high, fellow students began calling me "Quack Attack" for the T-shirt I wore about every other day. By that time, I was traveling with my dad to Autzen practically every game day. These were the days of Chris Miller, Lew Barnes, Derek Loville, and Bill Musgrave. It was Barnes' autograph I secured for my scrapbook, but Musgrave will always remain the player closest to my heart. It was in Musgrave's era the Rose Bowl seemed for the first time in my life a real possibility. Were it not for Musgrave's season-ending injury halfway through the 1988 season (his team at 6-1), I'll always believe No. 14 under center would have made it happen.

In 1990 I shocked family and friends alike by going to college on the East Coast instead of in Eugene. Although proudly green and gold to the core, I didn't want to choose a university based primarily on football. (Additionally, a juicy scholarship helped sway me toward NYU.) But rest assured, my Greenwich Village dorm room was wallpapered with *Register-Guard* and *Oregonian* newspaper clippings trumpeting Duck gridiron glories. As the Ducks made their astonishing march to the Rose Bowl in 1994, I became an honorary member of the New York City chapter of the Oregon Alumni Club.

On that fateful afternoon of November 19, 2004, we gathered at Lee Mazilli's Sports Café on the Upper West Side to watch the Civil War game that would propel the Ducks to their first Rose Bowl in 37 years— and the first of my lifetime. Other patrons gave us perplexed looks as we sang "Mighty Oregon" together in unison. (Better that than a Chuck Berry-style duck walk or ear-piercing duck calls.) After the game was over, I remember walking in the dark down 86th Street towards the subway, a rose stem clutched to my breast and tears rolling down my cheeks. When my dad and I stepped into the Rose Bowl stadium in Pasadena six weeks later, we both agreed this was what heaven would look like. When Rich Brooks' team ran onto the field at game time, the misty eyes returned. Oregon lost that game, but seeing them stay with the best team in the nation that year for three and a half quarters made me as proud in a loss as I'd ever been after a win.

Returning to my home state in 1997 to begin a journalism career, I at first shied away from writing about my favorite subject. Being a sports journalist demands impartiality, and with the Ducks that would always be impossible. However, once in a while I was granted a no-holds-barred essay. In *Willamette Week* in 2000, before the first Civil War game with both teams ranked in the top 10, I wrote, "I hope every team OSU fields in every sport loses every game. By a hundred points. Then I hope they run out of hot water in the showers and their bus breaks down on the way back to Corvallis." That was the sanitized version.

One behavior even fellow Oregon fanatics don't understand is the agony I experience watching Duck games on television. In fact, I've pretty much stopped watching them altogether. Instead, I tape the game and exhaust myself with housework or long walks to purge stress. After it's over, I check the score online to see if I'll be rewinding the tape to watch and keep or toss it in the garbage. It's come to this: I literally can't bear to see Oregon lose.

Luckily, though, losing is something the Ducks have done less and less often in the Mike Bellotti era. During the Joey Harrington years in particular, once lowly Oregon became the premiere team in the Pac-10 and one of college football's most consistent winners. When the final seconds ticked away in the dusk of Sun Devil Stadium on January 1, 2002, in the Fiesta Bowl, the tears rolled again. As the consensus No. 2 team in America heading into bowl season, Oregon was unfairly kept out of a national championship game that year. There is absolutely positively no room for debate on that matter. But kicking Colorado's butt in the Fiesta felt like much more than a consolation prize. As a *Register-Guard* headline read the next day, this was the "Crowning Moment" of a more than 110-year history. Some of the plays in that game, such as Harrington's pass to Sammie Parker or Maurice Morris' amazing touchdown run, are the ultimate highlights. (That era also had my favorite uniforms.) Even if there hasn't been a Pac-10 championship since, the great moments continue to come. In landmark victories over Michigan in 2003 and Oklahoma in 2006, I didn't cry—I ruptured my vocal chords screaming with joy.

No college football team can win and go to bowl games every year. Even Notre Dame had its Gerry Faust years. Sooner or later, perhaps after Mike Bellotti hangs up his coaching whistle, Oregon will probably face consecutive losing seasons again. But you know what? That's just fine. Regardless of scoreboards and stat sheets, no matter whether I'm in the stadium or covering my eyes and ears back home, the Oregon Ducks will always remain—outside of loved ones, of course—the greatest passion of my life.

Index

INDEX

Shanley, Jim 26, 27, 28, 29
Shaw, George xiv, 24, 25, 26, 42
Shedrick, Juan 97
Shehee, Rashaan 117
Shockey, Jeremy 159
Siavii, Junior 157
Siefert, George xiv, 55, 62
Siegel, Jared 149, 157, 164, 168
Simms, Chris 142, 144
Simms, Phil 142
Simonton, Ken 141, 151, 158
Simpson, O.J. 49, 50
Singleton, Herb 65
Sirmon, Peter 135
Sixkiller, Sonny 60
Skidmore, Owings, and Merrill 45, 161
Smith, Akili 121, 123, 124, 125, 127, 128, 129, 130, 133, 145, 165, 179
Smith, Hank ix
Smith, Jim 49
Smith, Jonathan 141, 151, 152
Smith, Joshua 119
Smith, Matt 139
Smith, Onterrio 121, 146, 148, 149, 155, 162, 164, 165, 172
Smith, Pat ix
Smith, Reggie 178
Smith, Richard 9
Smith, Steve 25, 149, 158
Smith, Valarie ix
Snyder, Adam 169
Snyder, Bruce xiv
Sorgi, Jim 148
Southern Methodist University 16, 20, 21, 36, 39
Specht, Greg 59
Sports Illustrated 35, 109, 128, 158, 168
St. Louis Cardinals 54
St. Louis Rams 80, 115
Stagg, Amos Alonzo 4

Stanford University 9, 25, 26, 30, 33, 34, 35, 41, 49, 51, 54, 55, 58, 66, 79, 91, 102, 107, 108, 116, 121, 124, 125, 128, 150, 177
Statesman Journal 123
Steitz, Nick 169
Sterett, Reese ix
Stewart, Jonathan 121, 166, 177, 179
Stoops, Bob 177
Stover, Ron 29
Stubler, Rich 120, 121
Sullivan, Corky 39
Sunia, Andy 84

T

Talbott, Tom 86
Tampa Bay Buccaneers 19
Taylor, Charles 5
Tedford, Jeff 127, 145, 170
Tegert, Lloyd 5
Temple, Mark 12
Terico, Mike 144
Texas Tech University 101, 102
The Daily Emerald 149
The Eugene Register-Guard 18, 38, 77, 158, 159, 182, 183
The Oregonian 26, 39, 64, 72, 79, 80, 86, 109, 139, 182
The Seattle Times 120
Thomas, Danny 39
Thomas, Osborn 76
Thomason, Jeff 98
Thompson, Paul 177
Thompson, Tommy 102
Toledo, Bob 88, 100, 115
Tomlin, Ty 151
Tourville, Charley 27
Troy University 31
Truman, Harry 21
Tucker, Marshaun 140
Tuiasosopo, Marques 139

Turner, Norval xiv, 63, 65, 66

U

UC Davis, University of California 115
Unitas, Johnny 25
University of Alabama 31, 44, 101, 131
University of Arizona 76, 96, 107, 108, 121, 129, 130, 134, 174
University of Arkansas 4
University of California 5, 19, 25, 27, 29, 30, 44, 55, 57, 66, 78, 80, 91, 103, 127, 150, 170, 171, 175, 178
University of California, Los Angeles 11, 16, 26, 27, 30, 54, 58, 67, 69, 72, 80, 85, 89, 97, 100, 116, 117, 128, 129, 130, 134, 138, 139, 164, 166
University of Chicago 4
University of Colorado 46, 73, 80, 81, 83, 84, 119, 120, 129, 130, 139, 153, 154, 155, 157, 158, 183
University of Florida 10, 169
University of Georgia 72, 74
University of Hawaii 51, 102, 104
University of Houston 77, 78
University of Idaho 27, 29, 30, 41, 46, 51, 138
University of Illinois 57, 59, 103, 116
University of Iowa 21, 91, 104, 106
University of Kansas 181

University of Kentucky 23
University of Miami 29, 107, 117, 154, 159
University of Michigan 18, 30, 31, 41, 55, 162, 166, 167, 168, 169, 184
University of Minnesota 135, 137, 170
University of Missouri 63
University of Montana 103
University of Nebraska 24, 25, 62, 82, 112, 154, 158, 159
University of Nevada 134, 137, 138
University of Nevada, Las Vegas 102
University of Notre Dame 47, 50, 75, 125, 131, 142, 151, 167, 175, 184
University of Oklahoma 19, 29, 55, 63, 67, 137, 175, 176, 177, 178, 179, 184
University of Oregon Hall of Fame 74
University of Pennsylvania 4, 5, 7, 8
University of Pittsburgh 23, 27, 40, 41
University of Puget Sound 4
University of Southern California 13, 16, 19, 24, 25, 26, 27, 29, 30, 31, 49, 50, 54, 59, 60, 62, 63, 67, 73, 75, 85, 101, 106, 110, 116, 118, 129, 131, 134, 138, 139, 149, 174

Celebrate the Heroes of Football & Oregon Sports
in These Other NEW and Recent Releases from Sports Publishing!

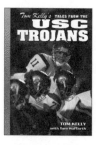